WINGLESS PEGASUS

A Handbook for Critics

WINGLESS PEGASUS

A Handbook for Critics

By

GEORGE BOAS

BALTIMORE: THE JOHNS HOPKINS PRESS

1950

To my Wife

PREFACE

A dozen or so years ago we published a short book called *A Primer for Critics*. It was an attempt to analyse and describe accurately the problems which critics of the arts and of artistry would face if they took their tasks seriously. It raised problems instead of answering them. It developed a vocabulary of criticism which its author naively thought might be adopted by the increasing number of people interested in aesthetics and the problems of aesthetics. Its attitude was what is usually called " naturalistic," its style literal. It met with a gratifying reception at the hands of a few literary critics, but was treated coolly by aestheticians.

In spite of all this, we have ventured to write a second volume conceived in the same spirit and dedicated to the same end. Our dislike for purple passages and fine writing has increased as the years have gone by and our love for clear thought and simple expression has increased. We have been led to believe that there is a growing interest in sentences which can be verified, whose truth can be tested by fact rather than by deep feeling. Ambiguity and vagueness seem to be getting out of fashion even in a field where they were evidences of profundity only a few years ago. If we are right, then our *Wingless Pegasus* will be welcomed hospitably.

But it is necessary to point out some of the peculiarities of this book. In the first place, its author's attitude towards the arts and towards artistry is both pluralistic and relativistic. It is pluralistic in the sense that he believes the word " art " to mean a variety of things and not just one thing; he believes in the real existence of arts and not of art. Nor does he see any reason why all arts should have the same purpose, be valued for the same reasons, be made under the same conditions. He prefers to speak of artists, rather than of The Artist. He also believes that the names given to the various arts and processes of artistry have been determined by historical and not metaphysical considerations.

That last sentence will locate him in the class of relativists. A relativist is a man who insists on stating as many of the conditions under which a sentence is true as he can find. He is therefore given to such words as " probably," " perhaps," and the like, for he is aware of his inability, especially in a relatively unexplored field, to state all the conditions under which his generalizations would be sound. But a relativist in aesthetics is a man who above all believes in the reality of time, location, history, multiplicity, and change. He realizes the difficulties of using common nouns and adjectives for things which have a temporal dimension, for such words by their very nature are non-temporal. When we use the word, *triangle*, we are supposed to be speaking of any triangle, wherever and whenever it is found. And similarly when we use the word, *picture*, we are supposed to be speaking of any picture whatsoever. But one of the most interesting things about pictures and other works of art is precisely what is conditioned by their dates and places. If one compare a Sung painting with a painting by some Romanesque fresco painter in Europe, it is not the fact that both are paintings which is interesting but the fact that both differ so widely. But of course if one is enamored of Unity, these differences will be minimized, if mentioned at all. One can always reach a level of higher and higher abstraction, if one wishes to, until one finally hits the realm of pure Being. But at that point everything is as true as everything else; to use the language of the schools, what is true about everything in general is true about nothing in particular. This book prefers to turn its attention to things, not to essences.

That is why there will be found frequent references to psychology and to anthropology, two sciences whose importance for aesthetics has been underestimated. Clearly, if all one has to do to understand a work of art is to gaze at it, then the sciences are useless. But if works of art are made by human beings living in different cultures at different times for different purposes, and not by disembodied spirits, then everything which we can find out about the human race and its ways of living is all to the good. We are more interested in men than in mankind; in fact, we believe that what is common to an Australian Bushman, a Polynesian, a fifth century Athenian, a fifteenth century Florentine, a nineteenth century Londoner, a twentieth century New Yorker, to say nothing of Cro-Magnons, Parisians of all times, and the makers of the Benin bronzes, is simply their bodies. But what they do with even this common property differs.

In order to keep the book simple and intelligible, we have indulged in repetitions, a kind of pedantic language, and perhaps even a regrettably didactic tone which will prove repulsive to some readers. But our experience in teaching and lecturing has led us to believe that even the most obvious statement in this field, couched in what might appear to be the most straightforward and unelliptic manner will be misunderstood by someone. We have sacrificed rhetorical elegance for intelligibility, which may turn out to have been a futile sacrifice.

We have also addressed ourselves to readers who have had some education and not to the rhetorical man in the street. The men whom we have met in the streets are not likely to be interested in our problems; they have their own to worry them. Therefore I have not felt the need of explaining, documenting everything, illustrating everything. The American reading public as a whole may be as naive as some of the book clubs seem to believe, but judging from the growth of museums and libraries, it contains large sections of serious and thoughtful readers who are sick and tired of watered wine and can take it straight. There are over two million college graduates in this country of whom at least ten percent. continue to be interested in ideas. It it to them that we are speaking.

Finally, it is with pleasure that I acknowledge my debt to certain individuals and groups of individuals. First of all, of course, to my students. Next to my teachers and colleagues, but especially to Professor Milton C. Nahm of Bryn Mawr whose criticisms have helped make this book less obscure than it might have been. Then to my friends, William Ivins, Jr., F. L. Lucas, from whose writings, both published and unpublished I have learned so much, to Lionello Venturi and the late Henri Focillon. I owe a special debt of gratitude for *obiter dicta* to Mrs. Susan Hoch-Kubie and as always more than can be expressed to my sister and my wife.

G. B.

Baldwin, Maryland
1947-1949

CONTENTS

CHAPTER ONE

PRELIMINARY DEFINITIONS

1. *Definition of artistry*

IF A SURVEY were to be made of man's desires, it would be found that they are satisfied in two ways: (a) by random, unconscious, "instinctive" behaviour, and (b) by controlled, conscious, intelligent behaviour. Thus a person in danger may either strike his fellowman blindly, throwing his arms about, receiving as many blows as he gives, kicking, biting, scratching, or he may use the lessons of the boxer, delivering his punches where they will be most effective, agilely dodging blows or parrying them, saving his energy. A person who is hungry may fall upon the first object which looks edible, devour it as it is, forgetful of whether it is good or bad, cooked or raw, too much or too little; or he may provide for himself three meals a day, think what his system needs in the way of a balanced and wholesome diet, grow his food and store it with an eye for tomorrow, to say nothing of providing for others who may be dependent upon him. On what may seem to be a less animal level, we find him sitting pencil in hand automatically scrawling shapes and lines which only a psychiatrist could decipher, or carefully reproducing some form which he has in his mind's eye. One may indulge in day-dreaming or in rational thought; in the free association of words or in neat and ordered sentences; in wild leaping and tumbling or in dancing.

This distinction is neither new nor recondite. Everyone

1

can observe its application for himself. No special theory of metaphysics is required to justify it. One has but to look for the events it differentiates to find them.

The control of behaviour as we are thinking of it is based upon awareness and purposiveness. Neither in itself is sufficient to mark it off from uncontrolled behaviour. Thus breathing and the pulsation of the blood may be called purposive, or eating, drinking, walking, fighting, sexual satisfaction, and so on; but they are not necessarily controlled. To control them, as we use the term, is to be aware of what they involve, of the purpose which we should like them to fulfill in distinction to their purely physiological purpose, to reorient them, if desirable, to ends which are not inherent in them but which we feel for some reason or other to be better than the purely physiological, to check them, to encourage them, to sublimate them. The control of behaviour therefore demands that we be aware of what we are doing, of what we want to do, of what we should want to do. It demands the submission of our desires to what has been called the Reason, or in other cases to the Moral Law, or the Traditions of Society, or the Voice of God, or Good Taste, or the Categorical Imperative, or Good Manners, or The Rules. It is such controlled behaviour which we shall call *artistry*.

Therefore two kinds of behaviour will be excluded from our definition. (a) instinctive, automatic behaviour, and (b) random, mechanical, routine, purposeless behaviour.

2. *The effect of learning*

As we begin to learn how to control our behaviour, we are aware of each difficult motor adjustment. The time required to perform the act in question is likely to be long. Thus in learning to play the piano, one has to be aware of the notes on the printed score, of the keys to which they correspond, and of the correct fingers to place upon the keys. In learning to dance, one has to be aware of the position of one's arms and legs and torso and of the transitional movements as one changes position. In learning to eat with a knife and fork, instead of with the fingers, in learning to walk up and down stairs, in learning to tie knots, in learning to read or to write, in any learning process, as the most superficial observation will demonstrate, one cannot skip the preliminary steps of careful awareness.

But as the learning process continues, the time taken to perform the act telescopes until it reaches a minimum. Processes which originally took minutes to perform, such as playing a simple major scale, now take seconds. The complicated process of writing a sentence, which originally seemed endless, now becomes almost instantaneous. But lest one forget the time which such acts once took, one has only to undertake the learning of new acts and one will re-live the experience. In the second place, the awareness which was needed in the beginning grows less and less acute. One sees the notes and one's hands fall into position on the keyboard. One picks up one's knife and fork and eats with them as if one had never gone through the painful and long process of learning to use them. One runs up and down stairs, ties one's shoelaces, picks up a book and reads, and to all intents and purposes is unconscious of what one is doing. The act once learned becomes automatic, as it were, innate, instinctive, part of one's being. So a person who has learned a craft is at a loss when asked how he achieved a certain effect, why he behaved precisely as he did. If he is a writer, or an orator, he is likely to say that he was inspired. For, having absorbed a certain manner of writing or speaking into his system, that manner has become second nature, as Aristotle called it. Whether the act be

in the field usually thought of as moral, or that usually
thought of as aesthetic, makes no difference. When the
technique of artistry is learned, it becomes " the " way to
behave. That other people may do it another way may be
admitted as a possibility, but not as a probability. One
has only to look at the manuscripts of such poets as Blake
to see that their inspiration did not exclude constant
revision. Their end may have been inspired, but not their
means of reaching it. And yet it is very probable that had
one asked such a poet how he reached his end, he would
have denied knowing. We have an analogy in ordinary
speech. Few grammars are more complicated than that
of English. Few languages have so unphonetic a spelling.
Yet we learn to speak and pronounce English grammati-
cally and in accordance with usage without stopping to
think each time we open our mouths. It is doubtful
whether any of us can remember our difficulties in learning our mother tongues. We see, however, children every
day struggling over what has become automatic with
adults. An adult might be found stupid enough to say
that his correct speech was innate. If so, he would be
similar to artists who have forgotten their lessons in
artistry. As one would refute the stupid adult by the
evidence of children, so one might refute the artist by
pointing to his juvenilia, if he had kept them, to his
sketches, his first drafts, his note-books. There are not
many composers who give such an air of spontaneity as
Beethoven. And yet his note-books reveal the great struggle he had with his craft, the numerous beginnings he
made, the almost countless revisions. On the other hand,
it is true, the manuscripts of Mozart, we are informed,
are clean and without erasures. But it must also be remembered that Mozart wrote in a highly formal idiom
which was drummed into him in childhood, so that once

his technique was absorbed, he had simply to apply it. Beethoven, on the other hand, was a constant innovator.

Not only does a learned process become short and almost unconscious, it also becomes compulsive, like any habit. We know that any act capable of being performed by the human being may become habitual, regardless of whether it be good or bad, useful or harmful, socially approved or socially condemned, approved by its victim or disapproved of by him. All that we can say about habits is that in their origin they may have satisfied a desire. But once the act becomes habitual, it takes possession of us and we have to unlearn it if we want to be rid of it. Those habits which are approved of become so compulsive that any other way of behaving seems unnatural. So naive people look upon cultures not their own as somehow barbarian, contrary to nature, monstrous, perverse. We see that in such a phrase as, "Any other way would be unthinkable. . . ." We are perplexed as children by the fact that other people speak languages which are not ours, that they eat foods which are not ours, that they dress in ways that are not ours. For generations the arts of primitive and exotic peoples were looked upon only as curiosities. In fact, one may say that except for Chinese porcelains, it was not until the late nineteenth century that any appreciation of exotic and primitive arts existed.[1] The perplexity and surprise on discovering that our customs are not universal may of course, and frequently does, lead to a kind of disillusionment. One may imagine that the early Sophists in Athens were so affected when they preached the relativity of morals. They learned from travelers' tales that Greeks, Scythians, Egyptians, and

---

[1] The writer was taught in school that even the Chinese were only semi-civilized, the evidence presumably being their cultural "inversions": men wearing skirts, women trousers, and so on.

Persians had radically different religious and ethical beliefs. They concluded from this that moral and religious values exist "by custom," not "by nature." They therefore seem to have spent a good deal of energy in ridiculing the customs of the Greeks. Their ridicule was to be sure misdirected, for a custom may serve a useful social purpose even if it does not exist by "nature." Customs are inevitable in society, just as habits are inevitable in an individual; that is to say, it is natural for men to develop customs. The fact that customs vary is important, but its importance lies in its suggestion that we ought from time to time to reconsider those of our society and see if they serve any useful purpose. It does not prove that we ought to get along without them.

3. *The influence of our fellows*

It would appear that if an individual were to grow up in solitude, he would become possessed of a set of habits which would be automatic and compulsive. He would never have the occasion to explain why he behaved as he did, for there would be no one to ask him. He would continue, like an insect, repeating the same performances over and over again, whether they were successful or not, useful or not. For he would have to. Any psychiatric clinic will provide cases of people who do things which appear to others nonsensical and harmful and do them under a compulsion as hard to resist as that of conscience.

No one, however, does grow up in solitude. There are provincial people, parochial types, who seldom, if ever, leave their communities. Such people absorb the manners of the little group with which they identify themselves and consider rebellion as monstrous.[2] But even in larger

[2] The newspapers recently (January 1948) published an account of

groups the customs of the tribe will seem inevitable, like natural law. Thus in 1879 a book of etiquette was published in which the following paragraph occurs.

There can be no question that the Creator, in establishing the institution of marriage, designed one woman for one man, and intended that each should devote their best efforts to promoting the happiness and highest good of the other. A plurality of wives has one invariable tendency: it debases instead of elevating woman; brutalizes the man, and brings untold trouble upon the offspring. Therefore Christian nations reject it, and cling to the law of nature and of God.[3]

Regardless of the intentions of the Creator, it is clear that there are more people who do not practice monogamy than do. What is more, we have reason to believe that the women in such communities feel in no sense of the word debased by the custom of polygamy. Prince Akiki K. Nyabongo, a former student at Yale, and well versed in European literature and history, in his *Africa Answers Back*, significantly dedicated "To My Mothers," points out how thoroughly the wives of a chief approve of polygamy, how they encourage it, how ashamed they are when their husbands do not have enough wives to prove their health and vigor. As for the matter of husbands and wives mutually promoting the happiness and highest good of the other, one must not overlook the words of Saint Paul, "Wives, submit yourselves unto your husbands, as unto the Lord. For the husband is the head of the wife, even as Christ is the head of the church. and he is the saviour of the body. Therefore as the church is subject to Christ, so let the wives be to their own husbands in every thing."

an 'Amish father who had kept his daughter chained to her bed for twenty years because she had refused to join the Amish church.

[3] *The National Encyclopedia of Business and Social Forms* . . . by James D. McCabe, Hartford, p. 89.

But to add to the discussion of our first quotation would be sheer ostentation. Reading it is enough to show how provincial it is and yet how deep the feeling which inspired it.

Even Mr. James D. McCabe, were he alive today, would probably write a somewhat different passage. For provincial types learn from others also. They absorb perforce the customs of their parish. To the extent that these customs are the satisfaction of some human interest, to that extent are the purposes of others unconsciously accepted by the individual. We obviously do not begin to think for ourselves until we have already been indoctrinated by our parents, our brothers and sisters, our playmates, our school-teachers. The fresh pure mind which seems to be the starting point of many writers on aesthetics and ethics is a figment of the imagination. Such minds may possibly exist at birth—though even that is doubtful—the child being not without some experience even in his mother's womb. But they certainly do not exist by the time they begin thinking about and practising the arts. Minds are trained at home, in kindergarten, in elementary and secondary schools long before they become aware of the existence of the problems which are commonplaces of philosophy. One of the great values of teaching is precisely the awareness it gives one of the emotional and intellectual set of one's pupils. They arrive at a university already convinced of the correctness, the naturalness, the unique rightness of ideas which their teachers have been questioning for years. And one of these, and the most dangerous to education, is that the teacher himself already possesses another such stock.

4. *The rise of novelty*

If such be true, how does it happen that any new ideas, new values, new customs ever arise? They arise through conflict.

Very early in life in modern society, in such countries as pre-Fascist Italy, France, Great Britain, and the United States, one becomes aware of conflict in the satisfaction of one's own interests and those of other individuals. Two people want the same thing and it cannot be divided. We have jealousy, competition, rebellion, that is, self-assertion. Or again, there may arise a conflict between the satisfaction of the purposes of one's own group and those of another to which one does not belong. On the political level, we have the People vs. the Non-People; conflicts between the interests of a priesthood, the aristocracy, and the military. On the religious level, we have examples of the conflict between Christianity and Paganism, between Roman Catholicism and the various Protestant sects. On the intellectual level, we find the " strife of systems," which may arise simply out of the perception that one's traditional ideas are false. That such non-aesthetic interests may have a profound effect upon art is exemplified by the current desire for an " American art," which can be best explained by the chauvinism current in this country between the two world wars. Other examples are the rise of popular imagery to the rank of " serious " art;[4] German romanticism as foreshadowed by Herder, a protest against the dominance of French taste. If one is aware of belonging to a social group and feels the compulsion of its *mores*, one is bound to try to obey them. When the moment comes at which they cannot be obeyed because of the pressure of a

---

[4] Cf. M. Schapiro, " Courbet and Popular Imagery," *Journal of the Warburg and Courtauld Institutes*, Vol. IV, Nos. 3/4, pp. 164 ff.

conflicting group, one is either forced to abandon them, to modify them, or to assume the new interest of exterminating the other group. When the French Protestants during the Religious Wars went about mutilating statues in the cathedrals, they saw these statues as the satisfaction of Catholic interests. They became the symbol of a detested religion. In their case no new aesthetic values were created, for part of the Protestant program was the denial of religious art. But in colonial America, Protestants did create an art of their own in the village churches which are still to be seen in New England. When a Marxist to-day writes about " aristocratic art " or " leisure-class art," he usually pleads at the same time for a proletarian art. Consequently two things may happen: (1) the conflict may arise in what would be normally called a non-aesthetic field and yet eventuate in novel aesthetic practices, or it may (2) simply eventuate in killing off the interests which are believed to be in conflict with those of one's group.

But no one nowadays in western society belongs to only one group. The child of five or six immediately finds his allegiance divided between home and school, or between different groups of friends. As he grows older, he becomes more aware of the conflict between his family and his companions outside the home. He learns that generations differ and soon also learns to speak of grown-ups as a special variety of the human race. There is nothing strange about the existence of such conflicts. And novelty is bound to arise when the individual tries to reconcile them. The reconciliation sometimes consists in little more than behaving according to the standards of the group with which one happens to be associating. This develops what from a " higher " point of view is called hypocrisy. But it is hypocrisy only if there is one group which has some sort of prior claim on the person's allegiance. So far

Western man has found no criterion by which he can judge to which of the many groups he must above all be loyal. One's God, one's parents, one's family, one's friends, one's sex, one's business associates, one's school, one's profession, one's country, all make claims upon one and each insists that its rights are primordial. As a Christian one is taught not to kill, but one's country drafts one into military service and teaches one to kill as efficiently as possible. One's parents demand on the basis of filial piety that one accept their beliefs; one's university teaches one with equal insistance that one believe in something contradictory. One's school tells one that its honor is the most important interest in a boy's life; one's friends sneer at this and urge one not to forego their company for the playing field. Old habits will not meet the purpose involved in these conflicts, for the old habits were not developed with this problem in view. Hence the individual must adjust himself as best he can and that best is a temporary and passing adjustment, a one-day-a-week acceptance of one set of habits, a school-time acceptance of another, an after-school acceptance of a third, and so on.

It is not maintained that such conflicts arise through the premeditation of anyone. The individual simply finds himself in a situation which his old habits will not handle. He thus perceives the necessity for change. But some conflicts exist which are deliberately instigated by a group or rather by the persons in control of a group. They are directed against other groups which they believe to threaten their power, prestige, self-esteem, or convictions, not that these four motives are exhaustive or inter-exclusive. Such deliberately stimulated conflicts are carried on by propaganda, sometimes well reasoned. A religious organization sees its existence threatened by some other group and sets out to demolish the other group. A trade union sees its interest threatened by a group of industrialists—or by another trade union—and sets out to demolish it. The privately endowed university sees itself threatened by the state universities, the public schools see themselves threatened by the private schools, medical practitioners see themselves threatened by socialized medicine, the farmers see themselves threatened by Wall Street, and Wall Street sees itself threatened by Congress. The list of associations and societies in the United States given by the *World Almanac* runs into the hundreds. There are associations of workingmen, professional men, actors, artists, antiquarians, athletes, atheists, patriots, nationalists and internationalists, sunbathers, veterans, merchants, sportsmen, the deaf, the blind, and the various fraternal orders. It is not beyond the bounds of plausibility that every interest in the country has an organization to further its satisfaction and to fight conflicting interests. A person who belongs to one does not necessarily have to fight all the others, but many of them he will obviously have to fight. It is not obvious that atheists and Catholics cannot live in the same country, but it is obvious that members of the American Association for the Advancement of Atheism are not likely to find much friendliness among members of the Knights of Columbus. It is also obvious, when one reads the list through, that many of these societies have overlapping and not conflicting interests, if one may judge from their ostensible programs. But one of their purposes is to continue to exist as separate societies.

There is in the third place the ever-present possibility of perceiving for oneself that old purposes which one has been trained to satisfy have become obsolete. For example, a changing environment will always present new problems which must be met intelligently, and a problem always arises when a change occurs. The change may not be great; it may be great enough simply to cause a feeling of uneasiness. But no environment is absolutely stable. Factors making for instability are well enough known to require no lengthy exposition. The most dramatic are natural disasters, like earthquakes, floods, droughts, or artificially produced disasters like the ruination of war or the sterilization of land through neglect and exhaustion. People living in environments which have been subjected to these influences clearly cannot go on living as they lived before. One who has seen the Silver Mountains of Dalmatia or some parts of the cotton-belt in the South know what havoc can be caused to land by erosion. The inhabitants of both of these regions have had to adapt themselves to a new kind of livelihood, which has entailed a change in all values.

But a simple growth in population may suffice to change the customs of a people. The density of population in Belgium, for instance, has made it necessary to find new ways of keeping the inhabitants alive. Had Belgium been a Protestant country or a free-thinking country, the population would have been checked in its growth by birth-control. A solution was found in manufacturing, but in manufacturing products which other countries would need and which would not compete with the manufactures of those countries. That is, Belgium turned as a whole to processing raw materials. It owns no raw materials of its own, to speak of, and it does not consume what it processes. It used to receive raw materials from other countries, largely from Germany, and sell them to other countries to be worked up into finished products. The history of Belgian enonomy during the nineteenth century is a beautiful illustration of how a people may meet the increase of population without either emigration, high infant mortality, or conquest.

Perhaps the most influential source of novelty, however, is contact with previously unknown peoples, either
through their entrance into one's country, as happened in
Holland after the Revocation of the Edict of Nantes, or in
America during the nineteenth century, or simply through
travel. The Grand Tour probably did more to stimulate
English literature than any other one cause. The influence of Italy upon England came about almost entirely through this sort of travel. Travelers, unless they
are like Cooks Tourists, are bound to observe novelty and
are confronted with the undeniable fact that other people
live differently from them. The clearest demonstration of
the effect of foreign influence is seen in cloistered societies.
Old China, Japan before the Meiji period, some of the
Pacific Islands, are perfect examples of societies into which
foreigners seldom if ever penetrated. Their customs and
ideas, their artistry, remained unchanged from generation
to generation. There were in all of these societies, with the
possible exception of the Pacific Islands, internal disrup-
tions which necessitated change, but the stability of their
cultures was nevertheless much greater than that of western nations among which interchange was frequent and
normal. One of the reasons for the relatively high degree
of stability in the Catholic Church is the pressure put to
bear upon its members not to attend the services of other
religions. Modern Russia is another example of a society
which seems aware of the danger of its peoples' knowing
anything of other people. The Iron Curtain is a device for
preventing such damages as would inevitably come about
through contact with the West. The West meanwhile does
everything it can to make the Iron Curtain a barrier to in-
gress into its domain by refusing visas and the like—and
no doubt from precisely the same fear that stimulates the
Soviet government. Cloistered societies have existed at

all times apparently and they are the most stable. One sees the same phenomenon on a small scale within a nation, in the clannish groups which are set up to remain isolated from the rest of the people. Old customs, old forms of speech, folk-arts, old superstitions, last longer in the remote country districts than they do in the cities. There is surely nothing astonishing in that fact nor revolutionary in pointing it out. It is again evidence that novelty does not arise spontaneously. City life is the life of various groups in communication with one another. One can live in a cultural solitude even in New York, if one makes the effort to do so, but most people do not. It is probable that the rapidity of artistic change that has come about during the last hundred years is attributable largely to urban life.

A fourth cause of novelty is what one can only call fatigue. It is not very potent and probably never acts in isolation from the other causes of cultural change. But in large urban centers styles in artistry change in part, at least, because people are simply tired of the old styles. It is to be noticed that fatigue is stimulated by merchants playing upon the human desire for display and pre-eminence and visible evidence of wealth. The whole complex of motives which Mandeville satirized in the early eighteenth century and Veblen in the early twentieth, can be used to introduce cultural novelties, particularly in the field of the arts. Changes in costume design, particularly in that of women, are certainly not introduced because they are necessitated by any changes in the life which people lead; they are introduced to make money for the clothing merchants. Were symphony orchestras managed for similar ends, there would be more novelty in the programs which they offer. But orchestral programs are made up for large groups of people, whose individuals traverse the social groups composing an urban population.

And since no money is to be made out of them anyway, it is safer to cater to the human love of the familiar.

A final cause of novelty in artistry is the very fact that the modern artist is an individual with varying degrees of skill and of perceptual acuity. Since he is likely to live in an urban community, he is in daily contact with a heterogeneous society. From the early nineteenth century on, men have developed a greater tolerance for diversity—if they had not, industrial society would have collapsed. So-called classicism is to a large degree traditionalism and it arose in small compact and relatively cloistered groups, such as Athens and Medieval Europe. One has but to read the criticism of Athenian society written by Athenians to see how much of the fault-finding was based on the notion that the old Athenian purity of culture was being corrupted by foreigners. But both the Greeks and the Medieval Europeans were great travelers and travel was bound to mean heresy. Both cultures, however, were dominated by a small group of people and heresy was stamped out in order to secure the stability of the tradition. It is sometimes maintained that the classical tradition has an inner equilibrium which was self-maintaining and modern writers who wistfully look back to fifth century Greece or thirteenth century Europe keep playing on this string. As a matter of fact, the execution of Socrates ought to be sufficient evidence that Periclean culture was not self-sustaining, and the purgative duties of the Inquisition ought to be sufficient evidence that the Church remained *semper eadem* by destroying anything which might threaten it with change. It is normal that societies seek self-perpetuation; no one can blame a group for not committing suicide. But at the same time no one ought to argue that a tradition perpetuated by fire and sword and hemlock has within it a principle of vitality which makes it eternal. The industrial revolution, in so far as it was a cultural revolution, necessitated the acceptance of change and of diversity. People who were discontented with things as they were consequently found a society more willing to tolerate their expressions of discontent. Artistic revolutions are changes in our way of doing things and in seeing new things to be done. Hence a long preparation is needed before such revolutions can become effective. The French Revolution may not have been caused by the Philosophers, but it was certainly prepared by them, that is, the popular mind was made ready to accept it because of their writings. So the Romantic Revolution was not caused by writers like Herder, but such writers made it more palatable to the public. One of the new concepts of Romanticism was that of historical periods. The sense of identity with the past disappeared when the historical sense was developed. It was possible for Breughel the Elder to paint a *Slaughter of the Innocents* and set it in a Dutch village. That would have been impossible for Delacroix.[5] But in the interval between Breughel and Delacroix there had appeared not only Herder, but also Vico, Condorcet, Voltaire and numerous other writers who emphasized the notion of periods, in which change, either for better or worse, had occurred. When a man like Daumier sees new things to paint, he will get his chance to paint them only if there is a group in society sympathetic with his point of view. There have been innovators at all times, but the acceptance of innovation has been more widely spread at some times than at others. The acuity of Daumier's perception was his own; it cannot be explained by the character of other people, by economic conditions, by Great Social Forces, or other external events. But the existence of Daumier's public can.

---

[5] See Appendix I, *Il faut être de son temps.*

Where would he have been without *La Caricature* and *Charivari*? And where would these papers have been without readers?

We have listed here a set of five sources of novelty in what we have called artistry. The list is probably not exhaustive, but it is sufficient to show that even sanctified customs can change. It should, however, be pointed out that none of these causes operates in isolation. A man is subject to groups of them which play upon him in clusters and in unpredictable ways. For every individual in modern society is a member of various social groups and is therefore torn by a conflict of loyalties and interests. This may not be true among the Polynesians, but it is probable that even on their islands there are recalcitrant men who grumble about the way things are done. Even monasteries, where there is every reason to expect submission to The Rule, there are refractory monks who have to be disciplined and there is no reason to suppose that around the council-fire in primitive communities the situation is any different. There is therefore no *a priori* solution of the conflict of interests and their satisfaction, no assurance of a happy ending to our social drama.[6]

---

[6] For the existence of recalcitrancy in primitive societies, see Ruth Benedict's *Patterns of Culture* and Paul Radin's *Primitive Man as Philosopher*. The testimony of the former is especially important, for the casual reader might imagine that she was arguing for absolute efficacy of the cultural pattern in its control of society.

CHAPTER TWO

VALUES

FOLLOWING Perry and Prall, we shall define a value as the satisfaction of an interest or desire. Anything which satisfies an interest or desire—and one might add " a basic drive "—is good, regardless of what tradition or subsequent criticism may say. Anything which does not satisfy an interest is indifferent; anything which prevents the satisfaction of an interest is bad.

1. *Interests*

By interests or desires we mean such experiences as hunger, concupiscence, aggressiveness, belligerency, manipulativeness, hatred, the desire to communicate with others, the desire to make fun of others, the desire to improve others. Each of these desires has an object which is usually external to the person experiencing it. We may hate or love ourselves, to be sure, and that is why the word " usually " is inserted. But since no one knows what the word " person " means, except as a grammatical subject, it makes very little difference whether the object is external to the person or not. The point is that interests and desires are what Mr. A. O. Lovejoy has called " respective " terms. One is interested *in* something; one has a desire *for* something; one wants to communicate *with* someone. One cannot simply be interested, as one can be satisfied. That is why we transfer the word " value " and its derivatives to the object satisfying our interest.

19

2. *The Criticism of value*

Objects supposed to be valuable are always criticised in the following situations.

(a) After the interest has been satisfied.

This appears when a person having desired something and obtained it, then says, " I should not have done that." The depression which often follows a satisfaction, *Post coitum animal triste*, may have a purely physiological cause. One may have eaten too much, or drunk too much, or tired oneself out. The painful results are seen to be effects of the satisfaction and the judgment of value follows. One loses one's temper and becomes aggressive and a feeling of shame ensues. One continues reading one's novel and neglects one's studies. One yields to the temptation to talk and discovers that one has made a fool of oneself. Before the satisfaction the unpleasant after-effects might have been foreseen, but if we begin at the beginning, that is, in childhood or at the threshold of a new sort of experience, we cannot forsee the results. There are usually plenty of other people waiting about to warn us, but if our interest is strong, we shall neglect the warning. Possessed by a strong appetite, as by a demon, one pushes ahead. At that moment there is no question of possible unpleasantness. One knows what one wants and one advances to get it.

(b) In other people

Unless we sympathize in the etymological sense of the word with our fellows, we cannot feel their desires. Consequently, we can tell them, as they tell us, that they are on the wrong track. By the wrong track we can only mean that the satisfaction will be followed by unpleasant consequences. To which the reply ordinarily is that no two people are alike, that one must live one's own life, that one must take chances, that one cannot make an omelette without breaking eggs, or any one or more of a score of similar proverbs. Such criticism cannot mean that the satisfaction of the other person's desire is bad, in the sense that it will not satisfy that desire; it can only mean that if his experience follows the same pattern as one's own, it will be followed by some effect which will prevent the satisfaction of other interests. One has only to read essays and books of edification to see this. When a moralist argues that one should not, for instance, be seen drinking in public, because, if one is, one's reputation will suffer, he is presenting to the person he is trying to edify a conflict of interests. He is not saying that taking a drink in public will not satisfy the desire to take a drink. Similarly if he argues that a drink will give you a headache, the reply may be that a headache is a cheap enough price to pay for the satisfaction of one's thirst for alcohol. A person is the only judge of what his desires are. He is often, indeed in general, a very poor judge of whether he should satisfy them or not. For desires are not self-critical. In fact, their intensity can be measured by the power they have to resist criticism.

(c) By perception of conflict between interests before satisfaction

There are, however, individuals who have been educated to the point of checking their satisfactions by the perception of conflict between a felt desire and other desires. It is as if the person were saying to himself, " If I do this, I cannot do that." So Antigone recognizes that if she obeys the law of the gods, she cannot obey the law of the state. She is represented by Sophocles as weighing the two values in her mind, and, it should be remembered, to a Greek obedience to the state was a sacred duty. Now no one outside

2

the theatre could possibly behave as Antigone behaved, for no one has that much insight into his motives or that much verbal felicity. But the task of the dramatist was to make her behaviour plausible and moving, as it was to make her sister's. The conflict of interests is thus presented in the sharpest and clearest fashion. Her behaviour stands as a symbol of an ideal condition, the kind of purified situation that one obtains in science, a sort of mathematical limit which real people may approach but not reach. No one can foresee all the consequences of his desires, nor even all those which might make him regret having satisfied them. But the situations in which people find themselves, and the desires which demand satisfaction are similar enough to permit rough and ready classifications. It is true that in simple and homogeneous societies these classifications will be more pertinent than in a complex and heterogeneous society. It is, for instance, easier to speak reasonably about "the Greek view of life," meaning Athenian life in the fifth century B. C., than it is to speak about the French view of life or the American view of life and make sense. Hence the ability to judge values on the basis of future consequences varies as a function of so many variables that it is not of the greatest utility.

3. *The ways of satisfying interests usually inherited*

The problem has a greater appearance of simplicity than the facts warrant because we usually inherit from the past the ways of satisfying our interests. These ways have become codified and sanctified by tradition. In America we usually satisfy our hunger by eating three meals a day instead of eating whenever we are hungry. There are, however, people who insert tea between lunch and dinner and even put in a supper at about ten o'clock at night—or did when food for supper was more plentiful. There are other people who, like animals, eat whenever they feel like eating. There are good reasons for organizing the satisfaction of hunger, but these reasons are relevant to our particular civilization, not to the nature of man. Similarly the desire to learn, whatever its pragmatic value, is satisfied in occidental countries through organized education, in most cases administered in schools which in turn are more or less supervised by the State. This has given rise to the idea that there is such a thing as " Education " which is different from the satisfaction of curiosity, that whether one wishes to know something, let us say, about the early English writers or not, to be educated means that one should know something about them. It is not difficult to see that the satisfaction of curiosity can be achieved without any schooling whatsoever—provided one has a good library and the proper laboratories at one's disposal—and that furthermore the history of occidental education demonstrates how different the proper subject-matters and the methods of teaching have been. There are plenty of items in the traditional American curricula which do not satisfy any native curiosity of the students whatsover, but have been retained in the course of study for traditional reasons and require constant apologetics from the teachers. The teachers, and sometimes public opinion, demand that an educated man know certain things and they may be right; but the satisfaction of the desire to fulfill the demands of public opinion is different from the satisfaction of the desire to know. If, for instance, public opinion demands that a university student have an intimate acquaintance with the plays of Shakespeare, there may be good reason for the student's studying the plays. But he is only accidentally satisfying his curiosity about Shakespeare, which he may or may not have; he is satisfying his desire in all probability to conform to certain social standards. Moreover, many societies include in their taboos a set of subject-matters curiosity about which is illegitimate. These vary from curiosity about sexual matters or military affairs or what goes on in executive sessions of the legislature to theological questions. Sometimes that which is illegitimate for one group is legitimate for another, the determining feature being age or sex or occupation. But it is easy enough to add to these complications and we shall not pile them up. The point has probably been made that the natural desire for satisfying curiosity is satisfied only within the control of society.

Hunger and curiosity are two fairly basic interests and the satisfaction of at least the former is essential if life is to continue. But equally essential is sexuality. If men were to live like the beasts, no restraints would be placed upon the satisfaction of sexual desires except that determined by instinct and force. But we have no record in the West, though this would not be true of some African and Oceanic societies, of communities which have permitted the free satisfaction of sexuality. Social controls have varied; some societies in the Occident have permitted with varying degrees of tolerance polygamy; some have forbidden it absolutely; some have permitted promiscuity in men but not in women; since the emergence of Christianity as the dominant ethos of the Occident, homosexuality has been punishable by law, even though not exterminated, and other aberrations from the theoretical norm have been severely criticised. But that our attitude is a cultural inheritance is proved by the very fact that the laws are necessary and that deviation from what the law permits is carried on in secret, arouses frequently a feeling of guilt, and when discovered is punished either by the courts or by social ostracism or some similar device.

But we see the same social control of the satisfaction of

our desires even in the field of the arts and sciences. Scientific method is largely taken over by pupil from master and its history shows how a technique which once was considered not only legitimate but uniquely legitimate is now obsolete. Even the problems of science are not necessarily original problems which have occurred to each person who tries to solve them. Aside from the obvious example of scholastic exercises which sometimes are little more than repetitions of famous experiments, one should not forget that at times the basic questions of science change. Thus up to fairly recent times it was assumed that Nature does nothing in vain and that consequently the fundamental task of the scientist was to state the purpose of every observable event. We are now so indoctrinated with the anti-teleological point of view that even when purposes occur, as in the case of human beings, we feel compelled to explain them as anti-teleological. In the arts, again, we know that what are called the eternal principles of, let us say, painting, have been in existence only for four hundred years and have changed bit by bit through these years until now it is extremely unlikely—one might even think impossible—for a painter like Raphael to comprehend the aesthetic principles governing—or resident in—the more recent painting by Picasso. Yet for years teachers of painting and critics of pictures took the academic point of view. It was not merely one of the possible points of view; it was the only correct one. When even so mildly novel paintings as those of the first Impressionists were first exhibited, the critics did not merely say that they exhibited a new technique of pictorial composition and coloration, but that they were the work of madmen, revolutionaries, immoral monsters.

These considerations give rise to the perception of a principle which might be called the Principle of Ritualization. Even though there may be certain interests which are universal, in the sense that every man must satisfy them if he or the race is to continue living—but note that some men have chosen death for both—the ways of satisfying them are not universal. They vary not only from time to time but also from place to place. Cultural history and anthropology will furnish the necessary examples. But within every social group certain methods will become the approved methods. In the dominant social group in most American cities, one eats three meals a day, goes to college, practices monogamy, approves of the experimental method of science, and probably prefers representative painting to abstract painting. If everyone in the European tradition had always behaved this way, we might conclude that it was the "natural" way to behave, even though a few of us might argue that it was only natural to Europe. But there is no way of behaving which has always been followed by all Europeans. We cannot therefore say that these compulsive patterns of behaviour are inherent in human nature.

We can more plausibly explain both their slow rate of change and their compulsiveness as an effect of the habitual. We know from our individual experience that the simple repetition of an act, regardless of its end, will eventuate into a habit, that the habit will become compulsive, thus seeming to be necessary, and that the ritual will be performed without reflection. We shall have more to say of this later on, but this will suffice here and now to illustrate how the satisfying of an interest will become ritualized. An example of ritualization which is not calculated to stimulate resentment is good manners. No one any longer believes that good manners are either homogeneous throughout all human societies, or inherent in the behaviour of any individual. They are something which one has to learn. They vary from group to group in complex societies, but in each group they are compulsive. Expressions of apology, of thanks, of sympathy, of affection, of dislike, are usually meaningless when analyzed or downright hypocritical, like the salutations of letters. (This should not be understood as condemnation of them.) They sometimes become burdensome to all concerned, like the letters of condolence which are both troublesome to write and to answer. But once the ritual has been established, it changes so slowly as to be almost imperceptible. It does of course change, varying slightly from individual to individual and from generation to generation.[1] But only the historian is aware of these changes. The man without an historical outlook thinks that the ritual is inevitable and right. One sees this not only in social etiquette, but in religion, in speech with its verbal taboos, its correct grammar, pronunciation, and spelling, in clothing, in the administration of law. It is of course the great stabilizing force in society.

4. *Instrumental and Terminal Values* [2]

There is a distinction in kinds of value which runs back to Aristotle and which we shall call the distinction between the values of those things which are believed to be good-for-something, instrumental values, and of those things which are believed to be good-in-themselves, the terminal. The adjective " instrumental " indicates that the values it qualifies are those of tools or means; the adjective " terminal " that it names the values of ends. The distinction is useful, but once made it demands restrictions and reservations.

---

[1] Cf. Paul Schrecker's *Work and Civilization*, esp. p. xvii.
[2] See the author's *Primer for Critics*, pp. 9-20.

The value of the means is irrelevant to the value of the end. For any thing or process may, and frequently does, have both types of value. Thus, if we use the words "good" and "bad" for the terminal values and "useful" and "harmful" for the instrumental, we have the following possibilities. A thing or process may be both good and useful, good and harmful, bad and useful, bad and harmful.

A beautiful picture would be good to look at, satisfying our sense of beauty, and at the time useful as pointing a moral, helping to decorate a room, being a good financial investment. A man who owned a Piero della Francesca might conceivably enjoy looking at it, and at the same time regard it as a bit of property which, if need should arise, would help him out of a tight place at some later date.

As for the good and harmful, Tolstoy and others who have preached the moral criticism of works of art have given numerous examples of this. But in non-aesthetic fields one can find others. For instance, when one drinks alcoholic liquors, one is satisfying a need; but when one discovers that one is drinking to excess, the measure of excess is the harm which the pleasure is found to entail. At the time of writing this (1948) there is a hue and cry against the *Comics*. No critic of the *Comics* objects to them on the ground that children do not like them, but on the ground that they have a bad effect on children for the very reason that they do like them. One might contend that oratory was an art which was good and yet harmful, in that its goodness is the cause of persuading people to act irrationally. But we are probably laboring an obvious point, for there are many fields of interest in which temperance is preached and temperance is always needed where the satisfaction of an interest is recognized as good but also as capable of having a bad effect.

The bad and useful has had more prominence in books on ethics than in books on aesthetics. Writers of theodicies have often taken the point of view which admitted the existence of evil but justified it on the ground that it was morally useful. Plotinus and some of the Stoics argued that poisonous insects and disease were useful, though bad, in that they taught men how to stand pain and suffering. But to take to a more *terre-à-terre* example, a picture dealer might hate the pictures which he found the most lucrative; or a hack writer might recognize his works for trash and yet find them extremely worth while; or a hypocrite might despise himself for his hypocrisy and yet indulge in it for its utility. That good ends are sometimes ·reached by bad means is surely an old enough story to require no illustration here.

The ideal situation is that in which the bad is harmful, for there we find no conflict, no hesitation in choice, no aesthetic nor moral problem. Unfortunately for the peace of mind of human beings, few such things exist. The out and out evil is like the out and out good, which is just what we ought to expect, given the varieties of human natures and that of the milieux in which they find their satisfactions.

5. *The emergence of terminal values*

This being so, the question arises of how terminal values emerge. We shall postpone for the moment the problem of whether anything is inherently good or bad and merely note here how things and processes acquire terminal values regardless of their original status.

By the Principle of Ritualization certain practices become habitual and therefore self-justified. The criticism of

a thing or process arises after the satisfaction of the interest which it is believed to satisfy. Criticism is usually
voiced by other people or by a person through his perception of possible conflict between interests. Thus anything
whatsoever which has instrumental value will gradually
acquire terminal value. In its early stage it will be justified
as being useful and the pleasure one takes in repeating
habitual performances, in recognition of the familiar, in the
smoothness and ease of performance—sometimes elevated
to the category of the efficient—is underemphasized. But
it takes time for a practice to be dropped from society and
obsolete instruments are retained long after their utility
is lost. One might have thought that after the invention
of printing, manuscripts would rapidly have disappeared.
But people who could afford them looked down on printed
books as vulgar and ugly, just as today people continue
to have their portraits painted, though photographs are
often, though not always, more lifelike. Manuscripts still
are used for ceremonial purposes; in the youth of the writer
of these lines, college diplomas were inscribed by hand on
parchment and were inscribed moreover in Latin which
few bachelors of arts could translate. Greetings from one
university to another are often handwritten on large—and
cumbersome—folio sheets, since they are supposed to be
more dignified than typewritten messages on small sheets.
Dead languages, like Latin or Hebrew, will be used in
religious ritual, though the congregations listening to them
cannot follow them. Some poets still use poetic diction in
their verses and consider certain words and phrases as
inherently unfit for poetry, however vivid and stimulating
they may be. Churches and American universities are
built in the Gothic style and are covered with architectural
details, machicoulis, crenelations, niches (without statues),
gargoyles, whose function is as obsolete as that of vestigial

organs on the human body. Fencing, like many other sports, is a dead instrument. The foils are tipped with rubber, the players protected from the very injuries which the practice was originated to inflict, and the whole purpose of the sport lies within itself. Slavery was retained in the United States well after the time when its inefficiency was demonstrated. The roofs of buildings which were originally flat, hipped, and so on for functional reasons, now are chosen largely for looks and even in northern countries where snow accumulates, architects will build flat Mediterranean roofs, because apparently they look more up-to-date. In fact, a good, but not impregnable, case can be made out for the thesis that the fine arts are simply those arts which have lost their original utility. If it be true that the paintings in the caves of Altamira, and the Valley of the Vézère were originally tools of magic, they would be good evidence in favor of this thesis. Certainly the dance, the drama, and much music were magical in their origin, but they have retained their place in society as fine arts regardless of that. But the most impressive evidence of the emergence of terminal from obsolete instrumental values is found in museums, such as that founded in Dearborn by the late Henry Ford, in which people simply look at all kinds of instruments, carriages, sleighs, furniture, lamps, which were all made for use, not primarily for beauty. Their beauty has arisen from the obsolescence of their utility. Or again, the furniture of the average American living-room consists to what might be a surprising extent of objects which no longer are solely useful, such as fireplaces and candlesticks and, for that matter, rugs. To complete the inventory would seem like superfluous satire.

6. *Inherent values*

It cannot be denied that the satisfaction of certain desires is inherently good, if we may judge from the behaviour of babies. But it is surely not necessary to expand on the fact that none of us can continue to live as babies for very long. Similarly Watson demonstrated—at least to his own satisfaction—that the sensations of dropping and of loud noises were inherently unpleasant. But the field in which we are interested is one which is occupied by adults and by the time one has grown to maturity the original affective nature of our experiences has changed. Even pain can be pleasant under certain circumstances. But nothing can be experienced in isolation from everything else and we are too sophisticated psychologically to subtract the influence of the *Gestalt*. Just as a musical note will sound differently according to the chord or musical phrase in which it occurs, so a color which in isolation might be pleasant, in combination with some other color might be decidedly unpleasant. But, as we say, since all of our experiences occur in some context or other, it is useless to try to determine their affective character in isolation.[3] One can no more say that the value of the whole is the sum of the values of the parts that one can say that the aesthetic quality of a sentence is the sum of the meanings of the words. If it were, the line

O sunflower weary of time

---

[3] As a matter of fact, how could any sensation whatsoever be produced in isolation? Experiments on the affective coefficients of the colors are of no value since the subjects are shown the colors in question against some specific background, and if one could expand the colored area to fill the whole field of the subject's awareness, that would again be a peculiar situation whose affective nature would be different from that of the same color in a smaller area.

would have precisely the same aesthetic quality as

O time weary of sunflower.

7. *Multivalence*

Not only may a thing or process have both instrumental and terminal value, but it may at the same time have several kinds of each. Eating is both useful for preserving life and also a pleasant pastime. The meal which one eats is a means of a cook's earning his living, or a host's entertaining his friends, of his friends meeting together for conversation, of a series of voluptuous tastes, sights, and smells, and so on. A book, let us say, *Pickwick Papers,* may be useful to a reader who wants to know something about manners and customs in early nineteenth century England, who wants to pass an examination in English literature, who has a lecture to give on English humor; it may also and at the same time be very amusing just to read, as indeed it is, and be read for no purpose ulterior to the amusement which is in it. Writing it may have been a pleasant occupation for Dickens, and at the same time an economic necessity. In fact, the inherence of a large number of values in anything would be obvious if theorists had not decided that one must forget most of them. But if one does not thus arbitrarily excise certain of the values as irrelevant, one is forced to the conclusion that anything may and usually does satisfy several interests. The situation may be summarized as follows. A thing or process may satisfy several interests (a) at a given time to a given individual. Example: I find that reading *Pickwick Papers* is both a pleasant occupation and prerequisite to passing a course in Victorian literature.

(b) At a given time to different individuals. Example: Reading *Pickwick Papers* is a delight to A and means of passing English III to B.

(c) At different times to a given individual. Example: When I was young I found *Pickwick Papers* a delight, but now I read it mainly to refresh my memory about the Victorian Age.

(d) At different times to different individuals. Example: To Dicken's publishers *Pickwick Papers* was a valuable source of income; to the reading public of today it is largely a quaint specimen of Victorian humor.

This situation is so commonplace that it ought to arouse no objection. But, as a matter of fact, critics and aestheticians prefer to believe that only one value is the appropriate value of a work of art—or even of artistry—and they tend to overlook therefore the multiplicity of values actually resident in them. Yet if anything, work of art or not, is thought of in its total social complex, it will be seen that univalence is never found. The author of this book was taught that money had only instrumental value, that it was valued only as a medium of exchange. But in reatlity there are people who value money for its own sake (misers) and others, more numerous, who accumulate it beyond all possibility of use. The latter will save money not to spend it but for a variety of reasons which would seem to be irrelevant to economics; the desire to be rich, the desire to acquire prestige by being rich, the desire to have power through prestige. One need not be a very subtle psychoanalyst to imagine the diversity of motives, other than economic, which would stimulate the accumulation of wealth. If one erects a theory of money which does not take account of this diversity of motives, one deceives oneself about the rôle which money plays in Western culture. Similar remarks could be made about *The Machine, The Army, Religious Ritual,* and indeed about every thing and act in which people have an interest.

8. *The interaction of interests*

The reason for this is that interests are not in actuality isolated from one another but interact. Their interaction may sometimes be harmonious, as when music is given a place in religious ritual, sometimes in conflict, as when the desire to be original proves a block to communication. One might plausibly maintain that though the *B-minor Mass* is too long to be used in a church service, the religious sentiment of the music enhances the meaning of the words. One could with equal plausibility maintain that if Mr. T. S. Eliot is trying to communicate an idea to his readers in *Four Quartettes*, his obscurity is a bar to the fulfilment of his desire. (He may, of course, be obscurely expressing an obscure idea, or no idea at all, for one need not merely express ideas in poetry.) Most human beings would seem to be a mass of conflicting interests, the spirit vs. the flesh, the desires for recreation vs. the desire for learning, loyalty to God vs. loyalty to Mammon, conscience vs. social pressure. It has been said that all such conflicts can be reconciled and that a perfectly integrated individual will result. It might turn out, however, that the perfectly integrated individual would have to live in a glass case through the walls of which no sound from the outside world would ever penetrate. For if it did penetrate, the perfect integration might be shaken and collapse. What is more striking is that in modern society there is so great need of integration, so great a feeling of conflict and even of frustration. For often a work of art arises out of that feeling and there is at least a minimal reason to believe that if all frustrations and possible frustrations were removed, no arts would ever be practised.

The cause of this is plain. Controlled and purposive behaviour is usually directed towards the solution of problems. But a problem is something which threatens to frustrate the realization of our purposes. By the principle of ritualization certain ways of solving recognized problems are set up and so long as these are successful, there will be no reason to change them. Artistry then becomes ritualistic repetition, automatic and compulsive. And it cannot be denied that much artistry is exactly of that type. What many " modernists " object to in academic art is its ritualistic nature, an objection which is only to the point if the artist is confronted by a problem which ritual will not solve. After all, few people object to grammatical speech, tempered with common sense. But grammatical speech is purely academic. It has to be tempered only when it is incapable of expressing what the speaker wants it to express, not simply incapable of expressing the idea but of stimulating the desired emotion. If now, an artist faces a real problem, which his predecessors have not faced, then the academic methods will no longer work. There is no known way of integrating or harmonizing conflicting interests, if those two present participles mean what they seem to mean.

9. *Basic interests*

But if human beings have certain basic interests which are common to all mankind and always present, then there are certain values which all men seek and should seek, if they wish to be normal. It might be argued that self-preservation and the continuance of the race were two such interests. But in fact they are not. For there are moments when saints and heroes refuse to satisfy either of these, preferring other interests which they are accustomed to call " higher." If it be maintained that the hero sacrifices his lower self to preserve his higher self, the thesis has force; but in that case a sharp distinction should be made before the argument opens between the kinds of self and the kinds of interest involved in their preservation. Similarly when a Neo-Freudian maintains that all satisfactions are sexual satisfactions and demonstrates it by invoking an hypothesis of occult sexuality, he is also guilty of the fallacy of ambiguity. It should not be forgotten that empirical observation shows that both of these presumed basic interests, self-preservation and sexuality, are themselves at times in conflict. The *débauché* is surely not very effective as a self-preserver or as a race-continuator. The converse is equally verifiable. Nor is there one universal way of satisfying sexual desires or philoprogenitiveness. It is quite possible that a given individual might be torn between these different methods.

The question then becomes one of choice and, as the old adage has it, to choose is to reject. The basis of choice ideally is rational, but reason too has its premises which by their very nature are non-rational. Tradition takes care of most of our difficulties and is not without influence on this one. But tradition itself in modern times takes two forms, one of which preaches allegiance to the eternal values, one to the theory of progress. The former may be called the technique of resignation, the latter the technique of rebellion. Resignation in action consists in deliberately accepting both customary interests as one's own interests and customary ways of satisfying them, however distasteful they may be. It makes for social stability and kindles in the individual a feeling of unity with his fellows which in itself is said to be pleasant and morally gratifying. Rebellion in action consists in substituting for traditional interests and satisfactions of interest one's own novel desires, in spite of their novelty. Such desires are not uncaused and have their genesis in real problems. Just as resignation makes for social stability, so rebellion makes for adaptibility. The traditionalist may at times be nothing more than a man who refuses to face the fact of change and insists therefore on the satisfaction of interests which are no longer vital. But at the same time the persistent rebel who is rebellious on all counts—if such a monster exists— is a man who becomes incapable of forming a program for life, for he is fearful lest the inevitable novelty of the future be too great for his tentative rituals. One can be obviously too stable and also too original, even though it is next to impossible to define the limits of tolerance in either case. The result is hit-or-miss, trial and error, muddling through, in other words the practical compromise so often observed with so little understanding in our society. But what else could be expected? We are neither Polynesians living on a simple atoll untouched with the influences of an outside world, nor monks living in a monastery.

10. *Fallacies in the determination of values* [4]

Of the many fallacies in the determination of values, we may cite the following.

(a) *The original value of a thing or process is the right value*

This is a form of chronological primitivism, which says that the original condition of things is the best and that consequently when we are looking for the value of anything, we have only to discover what interest it originally served and there we shall find it. This is analogous to maintaining that the real meaning of Christianity is to be found only in the words of Christ Himself, or in the primi-

---

[4] For the appearance of these and other fallacies in the determination of aesthetic values, see Wm. M. Ivins, Jr., " A Few Fallacies about Art," *Harpers*, August 1949, pp. 114 ff.; Sept. 1947, pp. 225 ff.

tive Church; that since paintings originally were representations of natural objects, they ought to be so now; that since men were originally beasts living in caves, without cooked food and but the simplest raiment, any desire for kitchens and tailors is corrupt and should not be satisfied. In the arts one finds this fallacy in the argument that since the first tragedies we know anything about were Greek, the tragedies of Shakespeare should be judged by the canons of Aristotle; that since the first houses were purely functional, modern houses should be so too; that since English was originally Old English (Anglo-Saxon), the use of Greek and Latin derivatives is bad; that since Bach wrote for a clavichord, the use of the piano in playing his compositions is to be deprecated. In short acquired values are illegitimate.

The briefest way of disposing of this fallacy is the simple demonstration that we are not primitive men and are acknowledged not to be very much like them. Consequently their interests need not be ours and hence their ways of satisfying them need not be ours. If a value is the satisfaction of someone's interest, it cannot be the satisfaction of someone else's interest. *A* does not slake his thirst by giving a glass of water to *B*. But since this demonstration may not be convincing to all, let us put the matter somewhat differently. If a given thing or process has a value, the technical question that must be faced sooner or later is whether it has that value as a particular or as the representative of a class. In other words, is the value of *Othello* to be found in *Othello* itself or in the class of works of art, *tragedy*, to which it is supposed to belong? It cannot be denied that when *A* gives a glass of water to *B* and if *B* is thirsty, then thirst is slaked. Similarly if *Othello* belongs to the class, *tragedy*, then whatever can be said about the class as a whole can be

said about its members, with the qualification that some
things can be said only about classes and not about members of classes. No one can deny that if *Othello* is a
tragedy in some intelligible sense of that term, then whatever can be said about all tragedies can be said about
Othello. So whatever can be said about all mammals can
be said about George Washington, Abraham Lincoln, and
any other human being. But there are also some things of
the greatest interest which can be said about individual
human beings which can not be said about all mammals
and the most important things to be said about George
Washington are not entailed in his mammalian nature. In
the case of works of art, the class character is usually
determined by their first appearance in history, a procedure
which is somewhat different from the usual procedures of
classification. That is, when a writer wishes to find out
what tragedies are, he is likely to go back to the earliest
tragedies rather than to take all tragedies and abstract
their common properties. Hence the derivation of the
values of a given particular work of art from the traits of
all works of art of its class, is vitiated at the outset, even
if it were true that for reasons unknown a critic ought to
confine his remarks to whether or not generic traits are
present in the particular under his scrutiny. For the genus,
one would imagine, must be made up of all its members,
early and late. Otherwise the word " mammal " would
mean only the first mammals to appear in the evolutionary
series, assuming that there was an evolutionary series.

(b) *The natural value is the right value*

It has been maintained that some of our interests are in
accordance with Nature and some are contrary to Nature.
Though " nature " and its derivatives have been shown to

be hopelessly ambiguous,[5] it is still argued that there is a natural value and an unnatural value in certain acts and objects. Thus it has been said that the natural value of food is the preservation of life and that any pleasures which we may take in eating beyond the pleasure, if such there be, in preserving life are to that extent bad. So sexual satisfaction as any other than the satisfaction of continuing the race has been also condemned. This fallacy was at the root of much so-called romantic criticism, which strove to reconstruct the natural man and to derive from his character a set of values. It could easily be shown by a variety of techniques that man as he lived in Paris, London, or New York, was in part a product of civilization and, since such critics tend to depreciate civilization, they maintain that the values of civilized man are evil. Attacks on luxury, on the heroic couplet, on the formal garden, on the seventeenth century French drama, on classical education, have all found a basis in this curious notion of man's being an unnatural animal who has become estranged from Nature. " Little we see in Nature that is ours," said that poet who is usually thought of as the chief of English romantics, though he also wrote two sonnets in defence of one of the most artificial forms of stanza which exist.

But until we decide upon a clear definition of the natural, we cannot apply it as a standard of value. In the second place, human nature, not non-human, must be our problem. If it is human nature to have an interest in the artificial—that is, to use its intelligence rather than its instincts in solving its problems—then the artificial must have value for human beings, however little it may have for angels, animals, plants, or hills and streams. The most

[5] See Lovejoy and Boas, *Primitivism in Antiquity, Appendix* (by A. O. Lovejoy).

consistent and radical form of this appeal to Nature as a norm is to be found in the Greek cynics, the result of whose philosophy was to eliminate all art from the legitimate interests of humanity. Since the arts are one of the most characteristic traits of human beings, the technique is self-refuting. We are looking for a determination of values which are human values; we ought therefore to reject any theory which denies that human values are real. There may be a kind of higher criticism, if the term may be abused, which will show the futility of the arts as a means to the good life. But a theory of values which starts by denying that most values exist is clearly of no help towards forming a method of aesthetic criticism.

Our remarks are obviously directed at those men who contrast the natural with the artificial. There is, however, a genuine interest shown by many men and very powerful, in simplifying existence, in rural living—which they mistakenly believe to be more simple than urban living—in meeting rather than avoiding material difficulties. When such an interest exists, its satisfaction is a value. But the satisfaction of one interest is not that of another, and hence if our interests fall into two classes, the natural and the artificial, the satisfaction of the former is irrelevant to that of the latter.

(c) *The value assigned by experts is the right value*

If value is the satisfaction of an interest, then the only expert is he who is being satisfied. If I am enjoying the sound of Dvorak's *New World Symphony*, I may be led to detest it by comments made by others, but while I am enjoying it, I am enjoying it, and it has value during that time. My second experience of it will be a new experience in that it is compounded with my memory of hearing it before. It may be a pleasanter or more disagreeable experience to me. It may be modified by having read the comments of other people, the experts in question. These comments may have pointed out to me things in the symphony which I had not noticed before. They may have compared it with symphonies which the experts as a group regard more highly than it. But there is common to the two experiences only my sense-organs and the air waves which eventuate in the sounds. The new elements, namely having come to it after having already heard it, having read comments on it, to say nothing of having lived between the two experiences, all these things and others will determine to some extent what I am listening for, and hence what I am hearing. They will consequently determine to some extent what satisfaction I derive from hearing it. An expert in psychology might be able to predict what my feelings would be, but he could tell me what they ought to be only in the sense in which the obligatory is the normal.

Since no work of art nor anything else has any value whatever unless it satisfies a human interest and since every work of art satisfies by being absorbed into a total human experience, and since each human being changes, it is hoped, as he learns and ages and grows, the total experience of a work of art will not be repeated as a whole in any one person's experience. In the second place, A's experience of a given work of art is not identical with B's, though it may be more or less similar. Unless the interests satisfied are identical, the values cannot be identical, except in the general sense of being either instrumental or terminal. Now critics, or experts, sometimes say very illuminating things about works of art which make them more interesting and more enjoyable, and in so doing actually change their value. But they do not determine

their value in the sense of discovering a hidden value
which is " really " there but unperceived.

(d) *The universal is the right value*

The word, " universal," as it is used in this context,
may mean one of at least two things: (1) that which
actually satisfies everyone's interest, (2) that which
satisfies the universal interests of man as man.

In the first sense, what is there which in fact could
satisfy the interests of everybody ?   Mystic experiences
are expressed in about the same language by almost all
people who express them; obscenity is almost the same—
though there are interesting divergencies—in all litera-
tures.   But is it likely that a Chinese who had never
studied English literature would find any satisfaction in
Hamlet or *The Rape of the Lock* or *David Copperfield* ?
For that matter, how could one translate the opening of
the Twenty Third Psalm so that it would be even intelligible to a non-pastoral people ?   That which might
satisfy the interests of all people in a tragedy like *Antigone*
might be the rhythm of the verse, but surely to argue that
one should think only of the rhythm of Sophocle's verse
when reading the *Antigone* is so peculiar an impoverish-
men of the play that only stubborn fidelity to theory
could make it plausible.   Certainly the Athenians who
saw it in the Theatre of Dionysos were listening to more
than that; Sophocles intended them to; and finally one
could beat the rhythm out on a drum instead of using
words and voices, and then one would hear it more
clearly.

In the second sense, if there is anything common to all
mankind, there would of course be an art of satisfying its
interests.   But we are not merely men, we are also Europeans, Americans, Baltimoreans, Christians, Methodists,

married, earning our living by selling shoes, poor, ambitious, and without children. Our specificities are as
powerful in determining our interests and the way in
which we satisfy them as our common traits. One might
extend the argument to maintain that only those traits
which we share with the beasts, or with the plants, are
the proper targets of the artist, and indeed much painting
and literature does aim at satisfying our purely sensitive
and vegetative faculties. Is there not every bit as much
reason to think of man as the whole individual man with
all his peculiarities and personal desires, as the person
who reads, listens, looks, tastes, and feels ? Moreover,
precisely what evidence have we that the universal is
better than the particular ? If we take the body of
European fiction, all that we can say that it has in common is that it deals with men, but the men it deals with are
so different that their humanity is not the main theme
of the books under scrutiny. Even if we particularize a
bit more and point out that both *Alcestis* and *Romeo and
Juliet* deal with love, we have barely mentioned the theme
of either. But for that matter, even when one play is an
imitation of another, as is true of *Hippolytus* and *Phèdre,*
the interest which *Hippolytus* satisfies is not that which
Phèdre satisfies. The differences between the two tragedies are just as important as their similarities. The in-
disputable fact that Phaedra is in love with her step-son,
common to both plays, is the least important thing about
them, if by "important" we mean that which makes
them of interest to us and that which made them of
interest to their contemporaries. The Athenian who saw
Hippolytus was seeing an historical drama in which he
may have believed, at least to the extent that we believe
in the story behind *Richard II.* But it was also a drama

of the strife between Aphrodite and Artemis.[6] Racine's audience may have generalized the story to the point of turning it into the tragedy of incestuous passion. But even to them it was not a morality play.

But the fundamental question is that of why the universal should be any more important than the particular. One of our problems is making our individual desires square with the universal traits of other men. It is true that much of our morality turns on this problem. We discover ourselves to be abnormal or eccentric or merely somewhat original. We are given by the social group with which we are identified a set of moral rules which we accept more or less easily and which by their very nature are supposed to be binding on all members of the group.[7] But we also know that many of our ideals, such as freedom of conscience, can be realized only by rebelling against the standards of the group and denying the social, political, sometimes the metaphysical theories which give them plausibility. But finally, the value of conformity to the demands of the group is not identical with the satisfaction of one's own interest, even when the two are not in conflict. Hence the value of the former can never be substituted for the value of the latter.

---

[6] To simplify matters, I deliberately overlook the two versions of the play, as well as its two sub-titles.

[7] Sometimes written, "binding on all mankind."

Chapter Three

MULTIVALENCE

1. *The three factors in evaluation*

SINCE WE ARE specifically interested in this book in the arts, we shall now turn to aesthetic questions.

There are three factors involved in aesthetic evaluation which must be considered before any theory of aesthetic value can be constructed. They are the artist himself, by which we mean the poet, the architect, the painter, the person, in short, who makes the work of art or who engages in artistry of any kind; the work of art or the artistry terminating in it; finally the spectator, an awkward word for the person who sees the painting, hears the music, reads the literature. No work of art, no artistry, exists in a vacuum. Each is as it is because it was made by a human being, living at a certain time, in a certain society, using certain materials. But it is also always part of someone's experience as an object of perception, and it is this person whom we have called the spectator. The spectator may be the artist himself who satisfies an interest in making works of art and also in some cases in looking at them after they are made.

2. *The artist*

The artist, to begin with, paints or writes or composes music to satisfy some interest. He has a purpose which may be almost anything in making his work of art. This purpose he hopes to achieve through his work of art. He is not just making random motions. The purpose may be his own, as presumably has been the case since the early nineteenth century, or it may be that of someone else, as when an artist carries out a commission.

But the purpose, whether his own or that of someone else, is not carried out in an unpredictable way. The artist will decide for himself, or will accept the decision of his patron, how he will execute his purpose. He will decide to write a sonnet, paint a landscape, compose a fugue, or he will accept a commission to do so, and the manner in which he will achieve his purpose will be more or less circumscribed. When the manner is highly formalized, he will stay within what has been known as " the rules," to be taken up in Chapter Four below. An architect's patron may simply order a house of six rooms on a given piece of land, costing so much and let it go at that; or the architect himself may draw for his own amusement the plans for a house of two rooms, of concrete, in a city block, facing south, costing as little as possible—though usually the restrictions will be much greater. A composer will decide to compose a fugue in strict accordance with the rules of Cherubini. A poet may decide to write a Shakespearean sonnet as much like Shakespeare's in form as possible. But neither the architect, nor the poet, nor the composer can decide simply to make a building (any building), a poem, or a piece of music otherwise undefined. His restrictions may be very loose or very tight, but they will exist, for even if a poet writes down everything that comes into his head as it comes into his head, one of his restrictions—or rules—is to discipline himself to the point of forgetting grammar, prosody, meaning.

The artist thus finds himself involved in a situation in which there are at a minimum three sources of value. They are the process of artistry, regardless of that in which it terminates, the contemplation of the work of art when finished, and, obviously, the effect of the work of art when seen by others.

The artist's interest need not be purely " aesthetic," as that term has been frequently used. It may be any one or combination of various types of interest: economic, ethical, religious, political. For the arts are instruments originally, instruments for satisfying real interests which real human beings possess. If one limit oneself to the so-called fine arts, a term which requires further definition, one will discover among other interests the following.[1]

Narration. Telling stories and listening to them have always been among the interests of human beings. Historians do little else. Stories may be told in literature, in painting, in sculpture, and even in music. Moreover, the interest in narration had been very wide-spread among people. The story-picture is no longer in style, though in some of the murals produced in America under the early F. D. Roosevelt administrations, it was revived. But many of the paintings, like the frescoes of Giotto, Raphael, Ghirlandaio, Piero della Francesca, Masaccio, are still admired by people who refuse to admit the interest in narration as legitimate in modern painting. I am not saying that the only interest of the painters in question was narration, but it would be contrary to fact to assert that it was not there and that it did not orient their artistry. The Life of Saint Francis, if it is to be told in pictures, must be present; certain incidents will have to be illustrated; and indeed some details, such as color, background landscapes, costume, and in fact the very placing of the figures in the composition will be determined by

[1] Cf. the author's " The Social Responsibility of the Artist," *College Art Journal*, VI (1947), no. 1, pp. 270-276.

the story. It is all very well for Matisse to say that he is not interested in what Giotto was narrating in the frescoes at Padua; Giotto was. And so was the public for whom they were painted. Hence one of the values which these frescoes had and still have is the value of the story.

Lyricism. A painting like Odilon Redon's *Head of Orpheus,* Henri Rousseau's *Dream,* Dali's *Puzzle of Autumn,* no more tells a story than a song of Shakespeare's does. What is the story which is told by *Come unto these yellow sands?* The words mean something, to be sure, but their meaning is not narrative. They, like the pictures mentioned, are related to certain pieces of music, which either arouse or express an emotion and the Italian terms, *allegro, maestoso, con fuoco,* and the like, which are terms indicative of sentiments, would be more fittingly used to describe them than terms like *The Decline and Fall of the Roman Empire, The Education of Henry Adams,* or *The Story of a Bad Boy.* In the case of opera, most people might be perhaps willing to admit that the narrative is of less interest than the arias. There are, to be sure, operas, like *Pelléas and Mélisande* in which the music is intimately related to the story, but there are others, like *Dido and Aeneas,* in which the libretto is downright ludicrous and the music a lyrical delight. Lyric poetry, lyric painting, lyric music seem at least to some people to be a legitimate form of the arts and to satisfy a legitimate interest of both artist and spectator.

Impressionism. By impressionistic art we mean poems, pictures, music, which neither tell a story nor are closely related with either arousing or expressing an emotion. That an emotion will be aroused by almost anything, from an algebraic formula to an automobile accident, is true, but its very truth makes it impotent to explain the target of all forms of art. The group of poets known as Imagists deliberately eschewed the expression of thoughts, particularly deep thoughts. There was a time when some poets believed that their descriptive poems must express a thought. Emerson's *Rhodora,* and Bryant's *To a water fowl* are telling examples. Neither Emerson nor Bryant, apparently, was able just to look at something and describe it. Were they afraid of emulating Peter Bell ? The rhodora had to suggest to Emerson that beauty was its own excuse for being; the flight of the water fowl had to suggest to Bryant that maybe God would guide him in life as He was presumably guiding the bird. But no one nowadays would insist that a poem like Bridges' *A Passerby,* or his *London Snow,* should be completed by a moral lesson. Similarly we accept pieces of music like Debussy's *Jardins sous la pluie* without demanding what it means, in the sense of what it is trying to illustrate. The impressionist, in his pure form, believes that sensory patterns are worth while in themselves, colors, sounds, textures, movements. If other things are associated with them, well and good. But the other things are by-products, not the main purpose of the work of art. After all, a good part of science is also pure description. A man may be interested in the binomial theorem without intending to do anything with it. It is a pattern, usually undisclosed.

Exhortation. But there are, to be sure, some people who want to do something about pretty nearly everything. One of the best examples in nineteenth century painting is Daumier, almost all of whose works are hortatory. He wanted to change people's minds, to give them new ideas about the Bourgeois Monarchy, about the *Beau Idéal,* about the classic drama, about snobbishness, about the legal profession. His caricatures and paintings are not merely criticism; they are criticism, plus lyricism, plus narration, plus impressionism. But no one can understand what is in, for instance, *Le ventre législatif* or the *Rue Transnonain* without knowing what Daumier is attacking. We once showed a slide of *La Rue Transnonain* to a group of art-students. They burst into laughter, thinking it a picture of a drunkard fallen out of bed, overlooking completely all pictorial details which might point to something else. Shelley's *Song for the Men of England*, again, would lose its force were it not understood as a hortatory poem. Similarly, patriotic hymns, religious canticles, bugle calls, are supposed to have and sometimes do have an effect on human conduct. All hortatory works of art are instruments for influencing behaviour, for ameliorating it, in the way in which Tolstoy maintained a good novel should increase brotherly love. Van Gogh felt much the same about pictures; he wished his pictures to make men more moral.

There are, to be sure, other human interests which the arts satisfy, magical interests, religious worship, making money, expounding ideas, and so on. But these four will suffice to show that one cannot speak of one aesthetic interest as exclusively served through the arts.

3. *The work of art requires interpretation*

The work of art is simply a dumb sign until it is interpreted. It is like a Chinese character seen by someone ignorant of Chinese, cloud formations seen by one ignorant of meteorology, children's cries heard by the childless, sea-shells, leaves, rocks, bones, all of which tell volumes to some people and nothing to others. But interpretations cannot be made in a vacuum. One has to know the syntax of a language before it can be understood, even when one knows the meaning of all the words. A picture which no one looks at is like a musical score which lies on a shelf in a library. It is dead, mute, incomplete, potentially a work of art, but only potentially.

But interpretation must be made by some human being, a human being who lives at a certain time, in a certain place, with a certain education, working from certain preconceptions. The students who thought of the *Rue Transnonain* as a comic picture of a drunkard fallen out of bed, not only did not see certain details in that lithograph—though it was shown on a very large scale, being projected on a screen—but since they were ignorant of French history and of Daumier's main occupation, they were looking for no social target in it. A person knowing no Japanese hangs up blue and white Japanese towels with obscene characters on them as pure decoration and is not shocked. A person who knows no Italian will listen to *Il Trovatore* and see nothing laughable in it. Since there is no stock human being who represents the universal, *Man*, artists have to put up with the human race as it is.

Now the interpretation of works of art will depend upon and vary with the following at a minimum.

(a) *The actual physical appearance of a work of art*

This changes very little, but sometimes extraordinary interpretations are made because of these changes. For instance, if the color which originally had been painted on Greek marbles had remained on them, would Winckelmann ever have spoken of their sightless eyes gazing at eternity ? The cleaning which the National Gallery in London in 1948 gave some of its Old Masters aroused dismay and delight in various spectators, as the new appearance emerged from the old. When it was discovered that mute *E*'s were frequently sounded in Middle English, a new appreciation of Chaucer's verse immediately ensued. But in general the physical appearance of works of art is fairly stable.

(b) *The interpretative tradition accepted by the interpreter.*

This is perhaps best illustrated by the people who, trained in nineteenth century academic aesthetics, took it for granted that painting must be imitative. Hence when faced with an abstraction, they were puzzled to know what it was a picture *of*. Since spectators are seldom purely spectators, but also praise and blame the works of art at which they are looking, the tradition accepted by them may make a great deal of difference to the value which they find in the work of art. First of all, there is the pleasure or pain to be derived from strangeness. Then, when a spectator, for instance, accepts the tradition of linear perspective, he will dislike and disapprove of a picture which does not follow the rules of linear perspective. No one approaches a picture, a poem, a building, a piece of music with an empty mind. He has learned from his teachers, his friends, the books he reads, that works of art should be interpreted in a certain way. He proceeds to see whether they can be or not. He is not always aware of his inherited learning and, when he is, is likely to imagine that it is not merely what *he* has learned, but is the correct foundation of all artistic criticism. He has absorbed it into his very nature and consequently cannot but believe it to be the inevitable and correct way of interpreting what is before him. Thus if two people with two different traditions observe a work of art, they will interpret it in two different ways.

(c) *The artist's intention as known to the interpreter.*
There is a tradition, which is commendable, that a spectator try to find out what the artist was trying to do and interpret his works of art in terms of that aim. It is assumed probably by such spectators that the first question to ask of a work of art is whether it has succeeded in realizing its author's intentions. If his intention was to tell a story, then the narrative purpose is primordial. If his intention was hortatory, then one must look for the lesson taught. The difficulty with this program is that (1) in many cases it is no longer possible to know what the author's purpose was, the author being dead; (2) the author's purpose at times is obsolete or so strange that if one's attention were to be fixed upon it, the work of art would seem merely curious. As an example of both difficulties we may take the plays of Shakespeare. We have no statement by Shakespeare of what was in his mind when he wrote *Hamlet*. Critics have argued that this was simply a play of chivalric revenge, a play concerning the Scottish Succession, a play showing the conflict between thought and action, a play expressing the incestuous love of a son for his mother, as well as other things. If Shakespeare had left us journals, notebooks, letters, prefaces telling us what he had in mind, our problem might not be so grave. We have to act as if the plays were self-explanatory. Again, Francis Mere, in his *Palladis Tamia* (1598) lists the *Merchant of Venice* along with the comedies, the *Two Gentlemen of Verona*, the *Comedy of Errors, Love's Labor Lost*, and the *Midsummer Night's Dream*. There is therefore some likelihood that the character of Shylock seemed funny to Shakespeare's contemporaries. This is also borne out by some of the passages in the play itself as well as what we know of how the character was played by various actors. Should we

therefore play Shylock as if he were funny ?   Or are we to
recreate the character, and hence the play as a whole, and
retain it in the repertory ?   For we can no more see Shylock as comic than we can see the *Taming of the Shrew* as
comic, though here enters no doubt an element of personal
prejudice. Can we for that matter feel Antigone's problem
as a modern problem except by deliberately overlooking
what was important for a Greek, namely, funeral rites ?
Can we again look at Van Gogh's paintings and interpret
them as his letters showed that he meant them to be interpreted, that is, as edifying instruments ? He maintained
that his reapers and sowers and fig-trees were symbols.
The very colors which he used in such a picture as *The
Night Café,* he says that he chose for their ethical significance. The contrast between the blood-red and the green
is a moral battle, not merely visual contrast; the soft
Louis XV green and malachite, contrasting with yellow
green and hard blue greens are supposed by him to
" express the powers of darkness." He says that he has
tried to express the idea that the café " is a place where
one can ruin oneself, run mad, or commit a crime." It is
one of the " ugliest pictures I have painted." But one
imagines that scarcely anybody of our society or date
sees all that in these brilliant and sometimes terrible
pictures.

(d) *The orientation of the interpreter's attention.*

Where then is one to look ? For scarcely any work of
art is simple. A picture has usually color, a variety of
forms, bound together into a composition, sometimes a
subject-matter, frequently a " meaning." A poem is not
only words, but usually metre, stanzaic form, literal and
sometimes figurative meaning, with the latter often on
several " levels." Similar remarks could be true of almost

every work of art, for even buildings have been held—by Mr. Lewis Mumford—to express something which is not simply architectural, but also social, political, and economic. Should the spectator confine his attention to one of these aspects and either reject the others or relegate them to a subordinate place ? Or should he attempt to find everything that is in the work of art ? There have been people who insist that everything which is not on the " aesthetic surface " is irrelevant. But on the other hand, the members of the Warburg and Courtauld Institute have successfully shown us how in some paintings and sculpture there are allegorical meanings in the iconography which helped make the aesthetic surface what it is. Mr. Wind's analysis of the iconography of Michelangelo's *Last Judgment*, even if only partly exact, shows us not merely things whose existence was unsuspected previously, but which actually influenced so apparently small a detail as the gestures, the position of the figures, the facial expressions. Mr. Panofsky's studies of Duerer's *Melancholy I* do not simply tell us what the various items in the picture symbolize, but show us why the figure is posed as she is, a factor in the aesthetic surface and certainly a factor which enhances the enjoyment of the engraving. Tolstoy with his insistence on works of art as instruments of moral edification, shows us how what he would call a bad novel or picture or opera may have a vicious influence upon us, regardless of the artist's intention. Plekhanov and other Marxian critics have done similar things. And Professor George Rowley in his studies of the principles of Chinese painting has indicated in detail how a very abstract metaphysical theory may not only set a subject-matter for painting, but also determine its composition and drawing. Whether one looks merely at the aesthetic surface, the iconography, or the social meaning of a work of art will in part depend on the tradition which the spectator accepts. But it is also true that some people, regardless of tradition, find themselves more attracted to one phase of a work of art than to others.

This appears in criticisms of such an interest as the history of ideas. Ideas have a way of appearing in various fields in European culture. An idea which might seem relevant only to ethics will appear in painting; and an idea which originated in physics will appear in philosophy. One of the best illustrations of this, best because of its familiarity and unquestioned authenticity, is the relationship between the scientific theories of Claude Bernard and the narrative technique of Zola. It has been the experience of historians of ideas that their critics believe them to be preaching the exclusive value of ideas in, let us say, literature, as if they were maintaining that because Courbet was a disciple of Proudhon, the only legitimate focus of attention in looking at a painting by Courbet were its expression of socialism and socialistic ideas. No historian, to the best of our knowledge, has ever made this claim for his work; the most he has said was that it made the work of art more interesting, by showing it to be more copious.[2] A copious thing may not be any better because it is copious, but men have a desire to know all that can be known and their interest in knowing, the *amor cognoscendi*, has a just right to be satisfied. The criticism against the historian of ideas thus turns out to arise from the automatic focusing of attention on aspects of a work of art

---

[2] Cf. the late Theodore Spencer's review of A. O. Lovejoy's *Studies in the History of Ideas*, and Mr. Lovejoy's reply. *Journal of the History of Ideas*, Oct. 1948 and Jan. 1949.

which are not intellectual, and the claim is made that they alone are the true, right, and proper focus. But it is overlooked that this interest itself is of relatively recent date and that there was a time when the reader of a poem, for instance, would automatically have looked for its didactic purpose. No one today would read Ovid's *Metamorphoses* as religious history or as the readers of the *Ovide Moralisé* read him.[3] We do not believe that Ovid was a Christian moralist writing allegories. Nor do we believe, as some of his contemporaries may have, that he was relating true stories. Our attention is directed to other things. That shift in attention is not inexplicable, but can be plausibly explained by all the historical influences which have been brought to bear upon us. At the same time we are not necessarily aware of these influences. Nor could any man live long enough to trace them all. We react to Ovid as living beings and our attention is directed by psychological causes which are by their very nature unconscious. Because they are unconscious, we may feel that our reactions are the " natural " reactions common to all mankind. Therein lies our provincialism.

4. *The spectator*

The spectator thus satisfies a variety of interests by looking at works of art. He may be sensitive only to the pleasures of the perceptual screen; he may enjoy the pleasures of interpretation, of expounding to himself— and to others—the meaning of what he sees, he may even

---

[3] The *Ovide Moralisé* as well as the use of Vergil's *Fourth Eclogue* in Christian apologetics are beautiful examples of what happens when people assume the homogeneity of the human race and their own typicality.

use the work of art primarily for ends which are beyond it, as when he uses it as an historical document, as a commodity to be sold, as an instrument for enhancing his prestige, as evidence of a theory of aesthetics. The value of the work of art to the spectator thus increases in complexity. Its ramifications extend further and further. He finds echoes in it of things of which the artist could not have been aware. He sees its own echoes in other things. The work of art becomes the focus of a variety of interests, their point of meeting. An example may make this clearer. Below is Milton's sonnet on his dead wife.

> Methought I saw my late espousèd Saint
>   Brought to me like Alcestis from the grave,
>   Whom Jove's great Son to her glad Husband gave,
>   Rescu'd from death by force though pale and faint,
> Mine as whome washt from spot of child-bed taint,
>   Purification in the old Law did save,
>   And such, as yet once more I trust to have
>   Full sight of her in Heaven without restraint,
> Came vested all in white, pure as her mind:
>   Her face was vail'd, yet to my fancied sight,
>   Love, sweetness, goodness, in her person shin'd
> So clear, as in no face with more delight.
>   But O as to embrace me she enclin'd
>   I wak'd, she fled, and day brought back my night.

It is beyond question possible to read this poem without any thought of its meaning, attending solely to the music of the verses, the rhymes, the stanzaic form. But it is also likely that most people reading it would perceive certain meanings in the words, the literary allusions, and, in fact, they could not understand what these are without going beyond the poem, not merely to Greek mythology, but also to Hebraic ritual. The last line, however, which some readers would believe to give the poem its poignancy, would turn into a metaphor and only the reader who knew that Milton was blind would realize how day brought back his night. None of this information is in the poem. It has to be brought to the poem. And a person who denied the legitimacy of exegesis from biography would have to maintain either that the sonnet was a failure because it was not a self-contained unit, or that he could deduce the poet's blindness from the last line. Since most readers read the sonnet with their whole minds, they will interpret it in the light of all that they know, and will not attempt to impoverish its meaning by deliberately and, I venture to say, arbitrarily lopping off relevance which is actually there. Is there not more reason for maintaining that this whole complex of associations is precisely the meaning which the intelligent, by which is meant the well-equipped, reader is bound to find made vivid and emotionally powerful in the fourteen lines? Clearly, if he does not know that Milton was blind, that his wife was dead, that Alcestis was brought back from Hades and why, that the Old Law demanded purification from the taint of child-bed, he will still derive some value from the poem. That could not be denied, for if he knew English, he could understand the words and sentences and presumably could read the verses with the proper accentuation. But what legislature has the power to decree that what can be conveyed to a mind ignorant of literary and historical allusion is alone the proper substance of literature?

We do not maintain by these words that the appropriate use of the sonnet is that of a document proving that Milton used to dream about his wife, was versed in Greek mythology and Biblical law, and fused his knowledge,

whether pagan or Hebrew, into his poems. That is indeed
one use which can be made of them, but only one. Again,
it is probable that the sonnet has been used by students
of Milton as an example of the Miltonic sonnet, as distinguished from the Shakespearean, the Wordsworthian, the
Keatsian sonnet. In the third place, an anthologist making up a collection of English poems, such as the *Oxford
Book of English Verse,* would no doubt insist upon including it in his volume because he would feel that it had
values which make it representative of English poetry of
the period.

How much of this Milton could have anticipated is
problematic. If the poem is sincere and Milton actually
dreamt of his wife and awoke to find her gone,[4] then it is
very likely that the poem was written with no thought of
its utility to anyone else nor even with any thought of
anyone's reading it. But Milton is dead and hence his
values can be ours only accidentally. We are readers, when
we read the sonnet, not poets, and we are constrained to
find in it what meaning it conveys to us. A generation of
American students not thoroughly enough familiar with
Greek legend to feel the emotional sting of the reference to
Alcestis will inevitably interpret the first quartrain more
vaguely than their fathers would have done. In all probability, if they read the sonnet at all, it will be because
their teachers have assigned it to them in a course in
English literature. Their interests therefore can be expected to differ from those of Milton and of his contemporaries. Nor is there any magic which will turn them into
Milton or his contemporaries. But assuming that they

[4] As a matter of fact, he had never seen Katherine Woodcock, his
second wife, with whom the sonnet is concerned.

enjoy reading the poem, their values will be real values, differing from those of other people because they themselves differ from other people. This may be called multivalence.

5. Multivalence in time

But since most works of art have a long history, the number of spectators can be arranged in a temporal as well as a cultural series. When this is done and essays critical of the works in question are read, it turns out that even when the essays are in praise of the works of art, their praises are based on such different qualities that to all intents and purposes the work of art has become a different object for each wave of writers. The critic like Vasari who saw in the *Mona Lisa* a marvelous representation of a woman's face is not finding the same values in that painting as he who like Pater or Gautier saw in it a hieroglyph, the symbol of "enigmatic womanhood." [5] Similarly the critic who sees in *Hamlet* a young knight impelled by the chivalric code to avenge his father's murder, is not reading the same play as he who sees in him— *vide* Goethe—the crippling effect of thought upon action. Works of art grow and change as their spectators change. And the history of works of art is to a large extent the growth in the number and kinds of value which human interest finds in them. Only by arbitrary fiat can one assert that one set of these values is the right set. The extraordinary fact is that works of art do have " that potency of life " in them which makes them of continual, if of differing, interest to men. Our Shylock is not Shakespeare's, our Phaedra not Racine's—nor was Racine's Euri-

[5] See Appendix II, *The Mona Lisa in the History of Taste.*

pides's; but similarly our universe is not that of either Galileo nor Aristotle; our society is not that of Louis XIV nor that of Philip of Macedon; our souls are not those of Samuel Johnson nor of Horace. To expect us to find in the works of the past the meanings of the past would be like expecting us to talk Middle English.[6]

[6] One of the most interesting examples of multivalence in my experience turned up in Brussels a month after the liberation of that city from the Germans. The Monnaie was putting on a performance of *Fidelio*. At the end of the first act, it will be recalled, the prisoners emerge from their dungeons and sing a hymn to the light and to freedom. The audience broke into cheers and wild applause and an old woman sitting next to me, tears running down her face, turned to me and said, *Vous savez, Monsieur, il y a beaucoup d'actualité dans cet opéra.* I realized at once that an opera which seemed to me the height of romantic nonsense, to the Belgians was almost straight realism. They had had husbands, brothers, and sons in jail, had gone to the most extreme ends to rescue them, and no longer saw anything ridiculous in this highly artificial opera.

CHAPTER FOUR

THE RULES

1. *Artistry and habit*

THE RULES of grammar, like those of etiquette, lose force as soon as enough people begin to violate them. No academy so far, no dictionary, no amount of propaganda, has been strong enough to preserve them intact. And yet we know from our training that there are certain rules in every field of interest which we do not usually break for reasons of which we are seldom aware. Each social group has its own rules which differ more or less from the rules prescribed in the books. In some there is an awful respect for what grammarians have said is right and proper, just as in the field of social etiquette there is a similar respect for what the *arbiter elegantiarum* has announced as good behaviour. In other groups there is a programmatic delight in breaking the rules and in developing rules of one's own which actually define the group which observes them by their very peculiarity, like the secret language of children or thieves' argot. But the person who is born into a group, and everyone is born into some group, absorbs the dialect, the pronunciation, the intonation, the vocabulary of his group before he becomes aware of the fact that it is not *the* way, the only right way, of speaking.

It is possible to write a grammar because a number of people follow the same rules. But the rules are first of all descriptive of the way people happen to speak. If it is

65

true that Dante established Tuscan as literary Italian, that fact can only mean that before his time Italians spoke a variety of dialects — as they still do — and that it was largely a matter of historical accident that Tuscan became standardized. The Italian before Dante, if he wished to write in the vernacular, could with equal rightness use Venetian, Pisan, Roman, or Sicilian, to say nothing of other patois. But after the time of Dante, according to a strict interpretation of Dante's rôle in linguistic history, he would be taught Tuscan as correct Italian and his local speech would become a dialect. It would be foolish to think that the process of standardizing a speech was as simple as all that. Influences from politics, religion, and so on were brought to bear on the change and in fact the change never took place in its theoretical entirety. But in so far as any such generalizations are true, this one will illustrate the process by which description turns into prescription.

Whether this occurs on the social or individual scale is of no importance. An individual's style is his habitual way of doing something, a way which has become compulsive and automatic because habitual. Just as some people never outgrow infantile manners of pronunciation, so a man moving to a foreign country after he has become adult never loses his native accent. He probably will not be aware of the pecularity of his pronunciation—nor sometimes of his syntax and choice of words—but the peculiarity will be there nevertheless and will be noticed by an ear which has not become dulled. But the individual, like the group, changes, meets new individuals from new groups, acquires new interests, wants prestige, feels uneasy at being strange, and thus slowly—and sometimes quickly —changes his desires, his manners, his speech. It is at this point that he will become conscious of having violated the rules. Returning to his old environment, he will be made to feel only too clearly that he is not the man he was, that he has forsaken the good old ways of his fathers, either through negligence or affectation, and is therefore reprehensible.

If artistry is the way in which we satisfy our interests, then what we have said will apply not only to the art of speaking, but to any art.

2. *The instrumental value of the rules*

By force of habit alone a set of rules will become not merely the customary way of reaching the end but also the best way. Good grammar is not revealed to children as simply normal speech; it is taught them as correct speech. Now it may be argued that for most purposes, we do not say all, speech which is effective in communication, which is clear and intelligible, has achieved its end. Sometimes such speech does not conform to the rules. But many speakers would hesitate to employ it. They would insist that good speech must not only be effective as communication but effective within the restrictions of the rules. Since few alternative patterns are ever given to novices, the initiate starts with the idea that there is only one way to reach a given end. That way becomes the right way and its instrumental value is accepted by demonstration. The way is thus frozen through tradition and teaching and followed because of the greater prestige which accrues to obedience. It was once pointed out by Hilaire Belloc in his book on Milton that sonnets on the whole broke in two at the end of the octave. The octave therefore was often used to state an alternative: "When to the sessions of sweet silent thought . . . ; " " Oft have I traveled in the realms of gold." The sestet then stated a consequent alternative: "Then can I grieve at grievances foregone . . . ; "

" Then felt I like some watcher of the skies. . . ." But, he also pointed out, Milton did not do this. Two conclusions were then possible: (1) that Milton had invented a new sonnet-form, had increased the extension of the word " sonnet," (2) that he did not write correct sonnets. Belloc chose the latter of the two possibilities. All he could have meant was that if Milton had been trying to write Shakespearean or Petrarchan or other traditional sonnets, he had failed. But of course he did not produce any evidence whatsoever that Milton had ever entertained such an idea. The question hence arises whether there is any obligation on the part of an artist to accept the habitual patterns of his predecessors. The history of art produces at least two extreme forms of artist, artists who faithfully do try to conform to past models, artists who care very little about that sort of thing and invent and experiment and strike out new styles and patterns of their own. In between there are various degrees of originality. There are thus two extreme differences in kinds of artistic, as distinguished from aesthetic, interest, the interest in exemplifying a traditional form, that of creating a new one. Beethoven in *Opus 18* was about as traditionalistic as he ever was; Beethoven in *Opus 132* about as inventive.

3. *The pattern acquires a name*

A survey of the various names of artistic forms shows that none is perfectly exemplified. No one always speaks in perfect grammatical style—if one did, what would become of the famous exceptions to grammatical rules? The rule that a predicate noun is in the nominative case is violated in so harshly criticised an English expression as, " It's me," which seems acceptable in so rational a language, however, as French. When grammar follows meaning, the rules go out the window. The English frequently use plural

verbs with singular collective subjects: " The Government
wish to announce. . . . " In French the following sentence
shocks no one: *La plupart des plats sont mauvais*; though
the subject is a feminine singular, the verb a plural, and
the predicate adjective in the masculine. Rules of prosody
are broken on every page of Shakespeare. In music,
Vaughan Williams, who certainly should know, says
that not " a single one of the fugues, either in the *Wohl-
tempiertes Clavier* or in the *Kunst der Fuge*, follows the
scheme of modulation which was afterwards prescribed by
Cherubini." [1] Examples could be extended. The rules thus
may be interpreted as ideal patterns which nothing perfectly incorporates or as names for patterns of behaviour
which no human being ever entirely follows. In music we
have such words as classical composition; in poetry, the
various standard metres; in the drama, the three unities;
in dancing, the five positions of the classical ballet; in
painting, the pyramidal composition, the three " grounds "
of the landscape, linear perspective. Rules are formulated
such as " economy of means," or " truth of material," or
" representative realism," or " unity of point of view,"
which may once have had a certain instrumental value,
but their instrumental value now is either forgotten or
overlooked. To take but one example, and that a very
famous one, in Horace's *Ars Poetica*, occurs the rule of
consistency of character, sometimes phrased as " Let
Achilles be always Achilles." [2] Now neither Achilles nor

---

[1] Art. *Fugue*, in Groves Dictionary.

[2]   Aut famam sequere, aut sibi convenientia finge,
        scriptor. Honoratum si forte reponis Achillem;
        impiger, iracundus, inexorabilis, acer,
        jura neget sibi nata, nihil arroget armis;
        sit Medea ferox invictaque; flebilis Ino;
        perfidus Ixion; Io vaga; tristis Orestes.
                                    Ars Poet, 120-126
The source of this is Aristotle's *Poetics*, XV, 1454b, lines 11-15.

Iago, nor Harpagon, nor anyone else was ever always himself. But after Theophrastus the theory was established that people could be classified into types or characters. These types historically were what might be called the Platonic ideas of human psychological kinds. The theory was doubtless allied to, if not based on, the medical theory of temperaments. Consistency of character made it easier for a reader to understand a character. Inconsistency might be truer to fact, but it was unintelligible. If then one's aim was to clarify the course of human behaviour and the inter-relations of human beings, to make them more comprehensible, surely a reasonable purpose, consistency of character was necessary. Moreover, it fitted in with humoralist medicine, as we have said, and consequently with astrology and the Aristotelian logical technique. But if one were beset by the unintelligibility of human behaviour and wished to present as vividly as possible the problems which spring from it—as so many writers do— then consistency of character was a rule to be broken and the critic would be foolish to insist on its observance.

4. *The ends acquire a name*

Artistic processes when ritualized become the best, the most successful ways of achieving certain ends. Since they cannot but terminate in ends inherent in them, as an egg terminates in a chicken, the works of art which are their ends acquire names and are standardized. We have then emerging at various times such things as the classical tragedy, the sonata, the symphony, the allegory, the Greek temple in one of the orders. If one is to obey the law of the three unities for some reasons or other, one will find that one has produced a classical tragedy. If one follows the rules of Fuchs or Cherubini, one will have produced a fugue. If one follows the rules of grammar, one will discover that one has been talking correct English prose. And if one never takes a step without first consulting the work of Mrs. Emily Post, one will discover that one has been exemplifying perfect etiquette.

But when one takes the works of art and the processes thus described and maintains that they and they only are the legitimate kinds and that all others are bastard creations of a disordered mind, one is talking nonsense. Their legitimacy arises from the assumption—and it is nothing but an assumption—that human behaviour must be such that it can be classified according to given headings and, what is more important, that all possible headings have already been discovered. It is presumably for that reason that some critics disapprove of the novel—a very recent invention—and of " nature-poetry." These kinds of literature arose late in the history of western culture and there were no rules already laid down for producing them. Consequently rules could be formulated only *ex post facto*. Some of them may be seen in the process of being transferred from other arts, as when the unity of time is taken over from the drama and Frank Swinnerton writes a novel whose action takes place in twenty-four hours; or when the singleness of point of view is taken over from painting and either a narrator or one character in a story is selected as the person whose perspective determines the manner in which everything is to be seen. But the novel has developed more freely than any of our other artistic forms, largely because there was no tradition sacred enough — thanks to its age—to induce writers to follow it. It is true that critics have inveighed against certain narratives on the ground that they are not " really " novels, but their protests have had little weight. Had Sophocles written narratives instead of plays, then critics would insist that Mr. Faulkner and his younger American colleagues imitate them. In fact, if novelists had the respect for the past that painters have had, and that theorists of a certain school say they should have, all novels would still be written as a series of letters.

5. *The disappearance of the instrumental value*

It has been said that since the harpsichord could not sustain a note, composers for that instrument devised the trill to do what the damper pedal will do on the piano. But when the piano was perfected, the instrumental value of the trill was obsolete. It was, however, retained in musical compositions, but retained as an embellishment.

If this be true, then it is typical of much that occurs in the history of artistry and the appreciation of artistry. The original rule is presumably formulated to reach a certain end, a type of drama, poem, picture, or what you will. But as it becomes absorbed into ritual, the correct performance of the rite attracts the attention and the interest of both artist and spectator and the work of art for which it was devised is forgotten. We have an illustration of this in sport. No one believes that the correct way of kicking a football and getting it between the goal posts is any more efficient than the incorrect way. Nor does anyone think that getting a ball between goal posts, either by carrying it or by kicking it is of any inherent importance. The game as a whole is what counts and the term, " the game," means the form as well as the end. (" Form " here means the observance of the rules.) Now a great many games are obsolete arts which originally may have had a vital importance, as fencing, boxing, and other forms of self-defence and attack. In fact, sport could be defined for theoretical purposes as dead art. None but the most naive psychologist would believe that a soldier could transfer the habits he has acquired in playing chess to the

planning of a battle. For though victory at chess is similar
to victory in war and the game is a war-game in origin,
to play chess means to observe all the rules and to fight
a real war means to improvise new rules. The form of chess
is not to be judged from the fact that one man wins. A
man may be defeated and yet play more elegantly than his
victor. Obedience to the rules themselves has taken on
value and the value it has taken on is terminal, not instrumental. Out of this situation arises a school of criticism
which maintains that this technical excellence is the only
proper focus of the critic's attention. That is not the point
of view of this book.

When one does take this point of view, a good or great
work of art will be one in which there are clear traces of the
rules of artistry. Our interest in the seventeenth century
French drama, for instance, may be confined merely to
this aspect of those very complicated and subtle poems.
We are more or less justified, for we happen to know that
the dominant tradition in seventeenth century France, not
merely in the arts but also in science and philosophy, was
self-discipline and that the ability to operate within restrictions was very highly rated. French society at Versailles, whatever it may have been elsewhere, was
thoroughly ritualized. That is a commonplace. To accept
the ritual, in manners, in speech, in painting, in architecture, in thought itself—witness the Cartesians—was the
great problem. Whether a man stands up or sits down in
the presence of his monarch is of no ultimate importance;
but to be able to do one or the other as prescribed and to
do it automatically, as if it were second nature, may be of
importance. Such rules are the grammar of living and the
satisfaction that comes of obeying them is neither illusory
nor trivial. There was, to be sure, in the seventeenth century in France a counter-movement of what may be called

—too loosely—libertinism. But that does not imply that the *honnête homme*, the classicist, the Cartesian, the Academician, the Poussinist, was either silly, " cold," or otherwise inhuman.[3]

6. *The formation of the rules*

(a) *The contribution of the material.* Whether one believes in " the truth of material " or not, one must recognize that the material with which one is working limits the scope of what one may do. One cannot make in unpainted marble what one may make in a picture and similarly there are things that one can do in a three dimensional statue that cannot be done on a flat surface. The modern dance which attempts to write essays on social conditions is limited to a few ideas or emotions until we shall have developed a language of gesture and posture as rich as that of words. But at the same time one can color a statue, as the late Romans did, by using polychrome marbles, or as the Greek and medieval sculptors did by painting their marble and wood. Similarly one can incorporate into a dance the spoken word. Here, as everywhere else, there will be found two opposing trends, one moving in the direction of severe limitations, the other in the direction of expansion of material. Bernini's *St. Theresa* has been harshly criticized as violating all the limitations of stone and bronze. The saint is represented at the moment of ecstasy, a transient, the most momentary of states; she is supported on a cloud which appears to be floating. And there are rays which are not material things descending upon her from Heaven. Assuming that Bernini was a sincerely religious man, we may infer that he was

[3] For the complexities of seventeenth century France, see M. Henri Peyre's *Le classicisme français*, which is indispensable for an understanding of this period.

hoping to inspire a religious attitude into the spectators of his monument. But he was also doing everything he could to overcome the limitations of his materials—which is also what a mystic does, if one considers his body as his material opponent. On the other extreme, we have a sculptor like Maillol. Most of Maillol's sculptures are so simple of outline that they form a single block, the only movement of which is in the planes and the silhouette. (There are one or two pieces of which this is not true—the Venus with the necklace for instance.) It would be absurd to attempt to judge Bernini and Maillol by the same standards of conformity to the limitation of materials. Yet both are nevertheless subservient to some of those limitations: neither's statues talk or move.

(b) *The human equation.* By the human equation I mean those limitations which are inherent in human nature, as we know it. For instance, in an art of communication, there are limits beyond which the work of art becomes unintelligible. The usual conventions of grammar, accepted through custom, are not an inherent character of our verbal symbols; they could be changed—and gradually are changed—and a language still could serve as an instrument of communication. But it is surely not strange to point out that by staying within the limits of grammar, one has achieved a maximum of intelligibility, whatever else one may have lost. Again, once the rules of Renaissance perspective were accepted as normal, spectators found it easier to read a painting in which these rules were obeyed than one in which they were not obeyed, and if one were painting a picture which had a subject-matter such as that of the life of a saint or an historical scene, which was of primary interest to one, then it was wiser not to present it in such a way that the rules of perspective were violated.

For the onlooker would immediately be so discomfited by the strangeness of what he saw that he would not see what the artist thought of fundamental interest. The laws of perspective were nothing more than one way of presenting a given subject-matter; that would be admitted by everyone who was neither a fanatic nor a believer in evolution, who might hold that the later was the better. It takes time to habituate the eye to manners of representation which are novel and if an artist wishes to use a novel technique, he must pay the price of being misunderstood. But in a period like our own, when novelty is not considered eccentricity, we have learned to adjust fairly rapidly to manners which are new. Judging from the history of artistic criticism, one might conclude that this has not always been the case, for the savage outcries against such relatively modest innovators as the Impressionists seem to be evidence that even their slight innovations caused the deepest pain.

All arts are not arts of communication. But presumably an artist who goes before the public expects a certain sympathy from it, sympathy in the Greek sense of the word. But one cannot sympathize with anything which is totally different from oneself. We sympathize with the lower animals, our dogs and horses, to the extent that we can humanize them; and I suppose one might say to invest the trees and flowers, the rivers and mountains with human traits, as committers of the pathetic fallacy do, is a means of expanding the human soul into cosmic dimensions. When we have thus expanded ourselves, we can find throughout the universe lovable and detestable features which tie us together with the cosmic scene. Hence when a poet is simply uttering a howl of pain, if he wishes to awake a similar emotion in his readers—but he may not wish to, to be sure—then inevitably he will observe certain rules. For his readers are not both babies and adults at the same time. They may be free of the prejudices of most adults; they may have a maximum of emotional innocence; but in the long run they must understand the poetic syntax of what they are reading if it is to have any effect on their emotions whatsoever. But whatever the poet's desires or his readers' incapacities, readers are human beings and thus are already formed by a certain tradition which will orient their interpretations of his words towards their sense and not necessarily his. There is probably only one art of pure communication, that of mathematical logic, so that what we say is not of the greatest importance. For even when we miss the sense of what a poet or painter or dancer or composer says, if the verb is significant in this context, we capture other things which we may like and approve of more. In fact, it may be true that some of us enjoy being tantalized by the obscure. To stand before a mystery and know that it is a mystery and yet refuse to clarify it is not completely unheard of in human history. The demand for intelligibility varies in strength, like every other demand, from person to person, and no legislation on the part of critics will diminish the variation.

7. *The value of the rules*

Since it has become customary in some quarters to deprecate the observance of rules—as if it were possible to perform any purposeful act without observing them—it is necessary to point out what instrumental value they have. They arise inevitably as the effect of ritualization and what is inevitable ought to require no justification. But there are one or two features of ritualization which are overlooked by its critics.

Ritual, though by definition a kind of restriction, a form of discipline, nevertheless is a liberation as well. For when one has learned to satisfy one's needs in a given way and accepts that way as right and proper, one's imagination is free to act within the ritual and to concentrate upon substance rather than upon form. There is, I suppose, such a thing as empty ritual, just as there are mathematical formulas. But no one, as far as I know, ever said that reading the empty form of a sonnet, for instance, was as good as reading its substance in the form. $A.b.b.a.a.c.c.a.d.e.d.e.d.e.$ is a rhyme scheme taken from a well known sonnet. It is not uniquely embodied in that sonnet, but occurs elsewhere too. If Keats accepted that ritual, absorbed it so that writing in it became easy, then he could give his attention to what he wanted to cast in that rhyme scheme and not be tormented with the rhyme scheme as well. This is beyond doubt an oversimplification of the writing of sonnets, but it will do as an example. The acceptance of ritual is identical with the acceptance of a grammar. No human act can be entirely new. The problem will be recognized as that of deciding upon the precise balance between what once would have been called spontaneity and mechanism.

Habit itself is ritual; so is custom; so is tradition. Since it is impossible to eliminate these three patterns of behaviour, we may as well master them. We are not maintaining that one should subordinate one's inventiveness or one's creative imagination to the rituals of one's teachers or those of one's social group, but some ritual will be established by the very fact that each moment of life is partly shaped by memory, just as the meaning of each word which is being uttered is given partly by the context in which it is occurring. It may be too bad that if we wish to speak French, we have to use what seem to us, habituated to English, like two negatives. But no one is forced to speak French. The imagination of a man who knows the rules of his language thoroughly is not impeded by that knowledge. On the contrary, he is freer to express what he wants to express for the simple reason that obedience to the ritual is no longer a problem. Ritual thus has the effect of being a tool with which one accomplishes certain purposes external to the tool. The trouble arises when people forget the instrumental value of the ritual and value it for its own sake.

But ritual also gives a kind of stability to a social group which presumably is desirable. It eliminates the constant plague of novelty. One knows what one can count on, as when in classical music one is prepared for the tonic by the leading tones. If one may indulge in a bit of speculation, it might be said that in a social group organized for invention, it would be desirable to have as much of life as is not immediately needed for invention highly ritualized. A person who is engaged in scientific experimentation or philosophic analysis, for instance, does his job better if he does not have to worry about his meals and the general economy of his family. His imagination is freed from dozens of worries which are the major occupation of the run of men. People differ, to be sure, in their tolerance of discipline. But to some men the strict obedience which is required in military organization is not painful but an opportunity for repose. So in factories, where working men are sometimes pitied because they have become part of their machines, it is sometimes observed that they thoroughly enjoy their absorption into a larger order of things, for it permits their imaginations to be lulled to sleep and their responsibilities to be reduced to a minimum. There are probably machines which all people detest; I have never found any. But what one does find is a hungry look on the faces of men who wish that they might be driving a huge steam shovel or an electric crane and who have to derive their satisfaction from watching others do it.

A more serious objection to ritual is that it impedes one from meeting new situations when they arise. We are tired of hearing about the generals who are always preparing for the last war. But the mentality which they exemplify is common enough. They are the critics who judge new works of art by old rules. When situations change, clearly human purposes are forced to change. One cannot work out problems in relativity physics with the theorems of plane geometry. I have seen American tourists who seem to think that by speaking English slowly enough and loudly enough they can make French porters understand them. Similarly there are critics of human behaviour who think that by strenuously asserting the old rules they can annihilate the accomplishment of new human purposes. One has, however, only to think of the history of marriage in the Occident to see how patterns change regardless of the critics and how even a ritual sanctified by religion will change when the living purposes of human beings change. Since society is stratified, there will probably always be people who will cling to the old rituals and actually believe that they are sinning when they develop, or have the temptation to develop, new purposes. It cannot be sufficiently emphasized that even in games new rules are usually invented for a reason, not from perversity. And in the more serious business of life, it is clear that the reluctance to change, which is a function of habitual compulsions, will prevent the rise of meaningless novelty.

Just as the strict observance of rules may completely frustrate a person who has to face a new problem, so strict veneration for the rules will prevent critics of works of art and of artistry from understanding—to say nothing of appreciating—what is before him. One may with reason

say that the social revolution now in progress is a battle between two ideas, one that production goes on for profit,
the other that it goes on for use. (I am purposely adopting
the slogans of the two sides.) [4] One simply cannot understand the labor movement, in so far as there is one in the
United States, by trying to appreciate its effects on dividends. It is not trying to increase dividends. Nor can a
protagonist of the labor movement understand his adversaries by attributing to them a desire to increase the
production and distribution of cheap goods. That is not
their purpose. So a critic who accepts the rules of nineteenth century academic painting will never understand
the painting of even Matisse—to say nothing of Miro—by
applying the rules which he learned in the Académie Julien.
Matisse, now one of the more conservative painters, has
never since 1905 tried to apply those rules. Nor is there
much sense in asking him to announce what rules he is applying. It would be wiser to look at his paintings and see
for oneself what rules they embody.

It is true that our relative freedom from established
rituals in the arts has produced, or at least encouraged,
a diversity of forms of artistry in all the arts, which is
sometimes called confusion. The confusion arises from the
assumption that only one set of rules is legitimate. But just
as Pope's heroic couplet would never have been adequate
for Shelley, though in Pope's time it seemed adequate for
Homer and Vergil, so the rules of Roger de Piles will
scarcely do for Mondrian or the later Picasso.[5] To main-

---

[4] Both seem to me to be annoyingly exaggerated. For what profit
would there be in producing things which had no use and which no
one wanted to use; and what use are profits unless they are employed?
But slogans are not invented in a spirit of sweet reasonableness.

[5] They can be conveniently found in E. G. Holt's *Literary Sources
of Art History*, Princeton, 1947. It is particularly interesting to see

tain that Mondrian or Picasso ought to have accepted the rules of Roger de Piles is also to maintain that they were entirely free to do what they pleased, a thesis which is scarcely true. For they were in part conditioned by their intuitions of reality, in part by their having been born in the end of the nineteenth century. But even if they had been entirely free, their choice of the rules of Roger de Piles would have been an expression of a desire to be faithful to a tradition. Roger de Piles had little understanding of either Michelangelo or Duerer, to take two examples at random. He never thought to apply his rules to medieval painting. As for oriental painting, his rules would have been equally irrelevant. They were thus in no sense of the word rules for painting; they were rules for making academic paintings of his time.

how painters rank according to De Piles (*Op. cit.*, p. 415). Giorgione is low in everything but color; Leonardo has the same total score as Giulio Romano and LeSueur; Domenichino outranks Poussin, Titian, Rembrandt, Tintoretto, Holbein, Veronese, Giorgione, Michelangelo (who has a total score of 37 out of a possible 80), Duerer, Caravaggio and Giovanni Bellini, to select only the better known names. However fantastic this ranking may be, the whole scheme deserves study, for when it is studied one sees not merely how relative to our time are our own standards, but how reasonable the standards of another time may be.

CHAPTER FIVE

FORM

1. *Meanings of the term*

THE WORD "form" seems to have been introduced into discussions of artistry by Aristotle. Aristotle had predecessors, to be sure, above all, Plato, and his term carried along with it a number of connotations which had accumulated during the period immediately before him. Now it seemed to suggest *shape* or *structure*, a meaning derived from its use in geometry, now the *general characters of a group* of objects, so that the species was the form of the individual members of the species, now *purpose*, as in metaphysical passages where the realization of the form became the end or final cause of change, now the *essence*, as distinguished from the accidents. These meanings are used interchangeably by Aristotle, for the metaphysical form was the purpose, the essence — in "natural" change—and the general characteristics of a class of things, all at the same time. In Aristotle's universe, things fell into fixed classes and understanding could proceed only by searching for those traits which they all had in common. He recognized the obvious fact that a class of things had some traits which were not shared by all its members; these, however, could be neglected, and were called the accidental properties. But since his technique of thinking was also teleological, he identified the general traits with the purpose and maintained that the universe was striving to approximate a perfect order and was prevented from doing so only by the presence of matter. In other words, there were two realms of being, that of Nature, which was perfect, ideal, without flaw or exception, mathematical in the sense of being logical, unvarying in its obedience to scientific law; and that of chance, which was imperfect, material, full of monsters, perversions, corruptions, exceptions, which could be observed but not known rationally, but more or less embodying the precepts of Nature. For scientific laws were not simply descriptions but also prescriptions.

The world of Nature or of the Forms was better to Aristotle's mode of thinking than the world of material things. It was better in the sense that fulfillment of a purpose is better than the possibility of fulfilling it. On the level of common-sense, no one would deny that our ideals are better than our performances, that the circles of geometry are perfect—being precisely what geometry says they ought to be—whereas the circles which are drawn on paper are imperfect, because of the crudity of our instruments. But Aristotle did not say, as far as we know, that any purpose was as good as any other; on the contrary, he distinguished between natural and unnatural—or artificial—purposes, between the purposes which Nature decreed as the inherent purposes of things and those which were determined by chance or accident. These natural purposes could be generalized as the making real of the essential characters of any potentiality. An egg may turn into an omelette or into a chicken; the former is the realization of an accidental trait of eggs, the latter of their essential trait. In Christian language, God made eggs to turn into chickens, man turns them into omelettes.[1] Now

---

[1] But since both the Peripatetics and the Christians said that animals existed for the sake of man, there was nothing wrong in breaking eggs to make omelettes.

the arts belong clearly to the realm wherein accidental
potencies become the purpose, or form, of change. Thus
in artistry, art imitates nature.

The ambiguities in Aristotle's use of the word for
" form " have survived and indeed become multiplied in
modern aesthetics. We have retained the notion that the
form is better than the matter, though we are usually not
so precise in our reasons why. At times " form " means
structure as differentiated from substance, as in the shape
of statues, the composition of pictures or music, stanzaic
form, or meter. At times it means structure as differentiated from content, as in a novel when we speak of the
plot as the form, the arrangement of events, the outline,
the interplay of characters, the *dénouement*. This may
amount to nothing more than the necessary differences
between an art which it takes time to perceive and one
in which time is irrelevant. One cannot read a novel as one
can take in a picture at a glance, and, consequently the
form of a novel must be strung out longitudinally. Again
form may mean the manner as distinguished from the
matter, as when we speak of form in sport, or style, or
etiquette. If we assume that an artist is primarily concerned with satisfying his interest in structure, shape,
style, and take over from Aristotle the theory that the
purpose is better than that which is a condition of satisfying it, and furthermore assume that there is a natural
purpose which every artist ought to realize, then we can
understand why form might be more important than
any other feature of a work of art or artistry.

2. *Inter-relation of form and matter*

But whichever of these meanings is chosen as " the "
meaning, it will be seen that there is so close a relationship
between form and matter that the distinction is good

4

only for purposes of conversation, and none too good for that. One cannot build a cube out of sounds nor can one give temporal dimensions to a painting unless one paints a scroll, as has been done in China.[2] That sort of thing would seem almost self-evident and we shall not pursue the question further. There is a subtler relationship which is more worthy of illustration. We choose from Latin poetry.

A verse from Ennius, cited by Saint Augustine in the *City of God* (II, 21) runs as follows,

Moribus antiquis res stat Romana virisque

This verse, like most verses, if not all, can be discussed from the point of view of the idea which it expresses and the form in which that idea is expressed.

In the baldest terms, the verse simply asserts that the Roman state persists because of its fidelity to its ancient customs and the character of its men. But so bald a statement is incorrect. For the English " fidelity " is only implied, not made explicit, in the Latin. In fact, one could with equal right maintain that the verse reads, " The Roman state stands firm upon its ancient traditions and its men." Or that it is based upon, or rests upon, or is built upon its ancient customs and its men. Moreover, however one translates *stat*, the English throws no more weight of emphasis upon the customs than it does upon the men. That emphasis is conveyed not by the words but by the position of the words, that is, by their arrangement in the line, by the form. The very meaning of the verse is thus tied to the verse-form.

---

[2] Though even here it is the eye which moves, not the actual painted figures. They pass before the eye, remaining stationary within the picture. The cinema gives us real moving pictures, but so mixed up with drama, that they scarcely count.

The verse-form is obviously an hexameter. But beside
the six feet, the dactyls and spondees, which could all be
beaten on a drum, the very syllables are arranged in such
a way as to intensify the meaning which they convey.
The line begins with two three-syllable words and ends
with two three-syllable words, and they bracket two
monosyllables. The persistence of the state is in these
two centrally placed monosyllables, *res stat.* But such a
mechanically arranged contrivance is not the whole story.
For the *res* is a Roman *res,* and the word, *Romana,* binds
the central portion of the line to what follows, thus preventing the verse from disintegrating. The suffix, *que,*
binds the *viris* at the very end of the line to the *moribus*
at the beginning, and it does it because both words are in
the same grammatical case. But there are still other
subtleties. In the whole line there are fourteen syllables.
The word, *stat,* which from the point of view of the idea
is the key-word, is the eighth syllable, occurring as close
to the middle as possible. But again, Ennius had two
choices for the position of his word, *stat.* He could with
equal formal correctness have written *stat res Romana.*
But in that event, the words equivalent to our " the
Roman state " would not bracket the word which we have
translated " persists."

If then one tries to separate the form from the idea
which it help express, one sees that one has done little
that is very illuminating. We do not happen to be
Romans. No Roman of the educated class would have
needed so pedantic a discussion as we have outlined here.
To him the position of the words would have been immediately effective, as effective as, for instance, the vocal
stresses to which we are accustomed in English and which
so often determine the meaning of our speech. One can,
if one wish, lay aside the meaning of Ennius's verse, the

idea, and consider only its form, but I fail to see what significance the form would have if one were not aware of the idea to which it was giving form. And by " signifi- cance " I mean its reason for being as it is. If our com- ments on the verse are correct, they explain in part why it is emotionally effective. But that does not imply that a Roman would have to be aware of all this plotting and scheming and contriving, nor does it mean that Ennius had to think it all out ahead of time. We may assume that Ennius was a capable writer of verse who had learned his art and thus wrote hexameters as if to do so were his second nature. It is not more wonderful that a Roman could write delicately balanced hexameters than that a mere child can speak Chinese or that an illiterate Ameri- can does not confuse " read " and " red " or " write " and " right." To read an English grammar is to have revealed secrets which one has known for years without being aware of them. But the unquestionable fact that one can speak one's mother tongue without being constantly aware of all the rules of speech does not imply that the syntactical and grammatical analyses of scholars are incorrect or without interest. Such rules are formal rules and they do of course possess a value of their own. They are interesting. So are the patterns of poetry or any other art. But at the same time, they are intimately related to the meaning of the material which they formalize and when they are given a kind of aesthetic priority over that material, a work of art becomes desiccated and sterile.[3]

[3] It will be amusing to Latinists to find Ennius, whom Ovid speaks of as *arte rudis* and towards whom Quintilian (*Inst. or.*, x, i, 88) is even more patronizing, cited here as an example of subtle artistry. But one may recall Dryden on Chaucer to see how taste changes in such matters. Ennius, moreover, was the first Roman to write hexameters and hence may have seemed more primitive to his successors than he does to us.

A similar exercise could be played on any work of art. But so many have been made, both of music and of painting, that it seems hardly worth while making more here.[4] For they all show that the form abstracted from the matter or the content or the meaning is an empty formula, a mold into which something may be made to fit, but which is of no value except as perceived when full. We shall return to this point later.

3. *The usual assumptions of formalism*

If it be held that the form of a work of art or of artistry is the unique element deserving the attention of the spectator, then it is usual to assume two criteria of good form as a basis of criticism. (1) The form must be *clear*. If one cannot discover the form, then it is as good as gone. But as soon as that assumption is stated, one of the major difficulties of the theory appears. Who is to be the judge of the form's clarity? People who are more than fifty years old can recall that even the music of Debussy was called formless and vague by Debussy's contemporaries, and indeed there are many pieces of music of the present day whose form emerges only when they have been repeatedly heard. The same is true of painting. A painting will be called formless simply because the critic is used to the standard forms of academic composition: the pyramidal form, the S-shaped form, the forms of symmetrical balance, and so on. I have heard a professor of English literature maintain that Bridges' *London Snow* was formless because he did not know the name of the meter in which it is written; and indeed the only meter it has is

---

[4] For two excellent examples, see Mr. Roy Dickinson Welch on Beethoven's third symphony, printed as a supplementary essay to T. M. Greene's *The Arts and the Art of Criticism*, and the various analyses by Dr. Barnes in his *The Art in Painting*.

that of falling snowflakes. It should be noted that there exists no matter entirely without form, even if it be a lump of earth. Form is like order: we recognize certain very simple kinds of order to which names have been given, like alphabetical order or order of magnitude or order of intensity, but after all everything that happens occurs in some order. I throw a coin ten times and it comes down *tails, heads, heads, tails, heads, tails, tails, heads, heads, tails.* If it had landed ten times showing *heads* or ten times showing *tails,* or *heads* and *tails* in succession five times, it would have been called an orderly series of throws. But the order which I have named is one of several possible orders of which there are 1024. Had the order which actually turned up a name, it would be recognized as an order and not relegated to the limbo of chaos. The real question is therefore not that of order vs. disorder, but that of an easily recognized order vs. one which is unusual. The partisan of form is frequently simply blinded by tradition, so habituated to the simply recognized forms, that he overlooks the possibilities of others.

(2) The form must be *simple* enough to be perceived. If there are forms which are so complicated that it is unlikely, to say nothing of impossible, for human perception to grasp them, then obviously they are worthless as elements of a work of art. For whatever else works of art are, they are objects of perception. The following sentence, if it is a sentence, is a case in point: " He loves his aigrette too with mainly did in most she could not newly instead dumb done entirely."[5] The naive reader inevitably assumes that the form of these words is that of an English sentence, but when he reads it, the form is too

[5] Gertrude Stein, " Christian Bérard," in *Portraits and Prayers,* p. 79.

complicated for him to grasp. Unless one has been in the confidence of its author, one is given none of the usual clues to deciphering the words. But there are other possibilities. The form may be that of a mind groping to express something about Bérard, thus reproducing a psychological process which is not adequately symbolized by the syntax of the text-books. Or the form may be that of musical sounds in which the words are devitalized, purged of their ordinary significance, and changed into pure auditory sensations. When words are put to music, we seldom object to repetitions, even when the fragments of sentences make little sense. In Bach's *B-minor Mass* two words, *Kyrie eleison*, are sung over and over by four voices. In the *Qui tollis* the altos sing, *Qui tollis peccata mundi, miserere nobis, miserere nobis, miserere qui tollis peccata mundi, miserere nobis, miserere nobis, miserere nobis! Qui tollis peccata mundi, suscipe deprecationem nostram, deprecationem, deprecationem nostram, suscipe deprecationem nostram, deprecationem nostram.* Almost any opera—and operas are supposed to narrate dramatic action—do the same, and everyone accepts the almost endless repetitions and scraps of sentences as a matter of course. But when Miss Stein wrote, "Cunning, cunning, quite cunning, a block a strange block is filled with choking. Not too cunning, not cunning enough for wit and a stroke and careless laughter, not cunning enough," [6] it seemed to be nonsense. And indeed it was nonsense, if we assume that she was attempting to write a normal sentence. But do we really know what she was attempting to write ? We know how beneficial her influence has been on some American novelists whose prose style has taken on a kind of vitality and truth to the actual rhythms of

[6] From " White Wines," in *Geography and Plays*, p. 210.

speech which the academic writers never achieved. And in such a book as *Brewsie and Willie* she herself reached an incredible approximation to living conversation. But whether she was aiming at this in her earlier books or not we do not know. In any event, the form of such writings was not simple enough for the average ear to catch and the formalist would thus disapprove of it.[7]

4. *The standards of formalism*

Out of the emphasis on form as a prerequisite of approved artistry arise certain standards. These are not the only standards which the formalist will apply, but they are the ordinary ones which he does apply. Pre-eminent will be *unity*, for though there are several kinds of unity— that of matter, of purpose, of origin, of content—a work of art which is not unified in some way or other will appear to lack form. The second will be *balance*, whether the equilibrium of masses which is exemplified in the symmetrical compositions of Raphael, or the kind of balance of good against evil, youth against age, male against female, city against country, which is found in many nineteenth century novels,[8] or the balance between octave and sestet in a sonnet, or the balance between what can best be called moods in a symphony, or the actual application of the laws of statics in sculpture. A third standard will be *harmony*, less easy to define than balance, because more dependent on the spectator's feelings. The term, as it is used nowadays, seems to be derivative from music, but we

---

[7] She may have been anticipating the form of the sur-realists who— see the paintings of Dali—have followed the dictates of fantasy or, if one prefers, the unconscious in making their pictures. It is obvious that Poussin would not have appreciated their results.

[8] See *A Primer for Critics*, p. 82, for suggestions of this sort of thing in Thackeray's *The Virginians*.

know that musical harmony, as contrasted with discord, though originally based on the physical traits of air-waves, now has become a matter of feeling and even in popular music there are intervals which in classical music would have been denounced as illegitimate discords. What a person feels to be discordant will depend largely on his preconceptions, on what he is used to. The use of pure colors in unusual juxtaposition by Matisse is now accepted not only as legitimate, but as beautiful, and the rapid shift of tone in poetry which one found startling in Jules Laforgue, now seems normal—and perhaps even a bit banal—in Mr. Eliot. If Leconte de Lisle is harmonious, then Laforgue is discordant, and if harmony is an essential of poetry, then the verses of Laforgue are not poetic. But regardless of the name which one gives them, we wish to read them and we enjoy them and they stir us deeply—much more than those of Leconte de Lisle. Our conclusion will probably be either that harmony is not an essential trait of poetry or that we don't care much about poetry. Finally, the formalist is likely to invoke the standard of *coherence,* which produces a kind of unity, the unity of an organism. The organismic theory of works of art is an old one, appearing clearly in Plato's *Phaedrus,* where it is applied to oratory, and made more general in Aristotle's *Poetics.* The standard of coherence, however, can be applied literally only to certain works of art. It is all very well to say that a drama or a speech must have a beginning, a middle, and an end, as a life-history has, but how can one say the same of a picture, except in some highly metaphorical sense ? Moreover, the coherence of life is little more than what is expressed in the truism that living beings are born, mature, and die. In the case of animals and plants, of whose inner life we know nothing, the design of the life-cycle seems clear enough, standardized enough to be universal. But in the case of human beings, the life-cycle is the least of our problems, so small a problem that thousands of people refuse to admit that we die. The problems of life may consist, and do consist in many biographies, in the struggle to attain to some coherence, and who has the power to decree that a novelist or a dramatist may not depict that struggle ? The human body is certainly coherent, disposed symmetrically about a verticle axis and functionally, when healthy, operating as a whole.[9] But the human soul is a battle-ground of of conflicting desires, ambitions, hopes, in which frustration is as common, however undesirable, as harmony.

4. *Mechanism vs. spontaneity*

The standards of formalism given above apply most literally to machines. And the classic rules of art, those of sixteenth century and nineteenth century academic painting, of the seventeenth century French drama, of French architecture as taught at the Beaux-Arts and illustrated in such a building as Garnier's *Opéra*, have been actually followed and have produced works of art which, even though sneered at today by the *avant-garde*, have excited the admiration of not the least intelligent members of the human race. It is true that their taste is not ours. The rating given by Roger de Piles, of which we have spoken in Chapter Four, does not concur with the rating which most of us would give today, assuming that we should be foolish enough to rate pictures on a mathematical scale. But Roger de Piles was ranking his painters of the four counts of composition, drawing, color, and expression and where he fails to agree with modern taste is

---

[9] As a matter of brute fact, even somatic coherence can be over-emphasized. There is a war between the members well down on the " instinctive " level.

in his overlooking the interplay between mechanical perfection and what some writers of the early nineteenth century called " spontaneity." The Romantic Movement
taught men to look for a balance of opposite traits in a
work of art, to think of mechanical balance as cold and
lifeless and to prefer the warm and vital. It thought, as
Victor Hugo maintained in his preface to *Cromwell,* that
works of art must illustrate the union of the sublime and
the absurd, a union which to one philosopher at least,
Schelling, was characteristic of the universe as a whole.
But the earlier centuries were not so enamored of life as
we are. The sciences of biology, psychology, and anthropology had not been developed and consequently could
not have the prestige which they have today. That the
standards of that time were different from ours is thus
explicable and to be expected.

Once the interplay of the mechanical with the spontaneous is admitted, we begin to demand that the unity
of a work of art be played against variety: as Whistler
once remarked, a symphony in F is not simply F, F, F, F.
. . . We shall in the second place demand that balance
be not merely the equilibrium of opposing masses, but
that of opposing forces or thrusts, that the harmony be
that of at least a threatened discord, and that the coherence be that of disparate elements. We thus introduce
into all the arts a characteristic of one of them, the drama,
and look for an *agon,* a struggle, if not overt, at any rate
suggested. It was probably the introduction of this
standard which brought about in all the arts the new
admiration for the painters and sculptors of the Baroque,
though of course it took years for the new standard to
makes itself felt in all fields. The natural development of
the tendency became clear when struggle, dynamism,
movement, variety, and finally the release of artistry from

something called *The Reason* were sought for. At that point critics became aware that the notion of formalism had to be corrected, that form abstracted from matter was not sufficient for artistic pleasure, but that it must be perceived embedded in the matter.

5. *Dynamic vs. static form*

Regardless of the logic of the situation, and few critics were very clear about their fundamental principles, the balance between the dynamic and the static, between mechanism and spontaneity, was forgotten in some quarters and the dynamic was praised at the expense of the static. The nineteenth century saw the emergence of the biological sciences as natural sciences, out of their primordial source in speculative metaphysics. Their problems became submissive to the experimental technique and after 1828, when urea was synthesized, it could no longer be held that organic compounds could be produced only by the Life-Force. For there was no Life-Force in a test-tube. Moreover, this was the period when even the fixed species of organisms were found to have evolved, and the evolutionary metaphor was used by Spencer and his school to describe pretty nearly everything, social history, ideas, art, the stellar universe. Time became recognized as a creator as well as a destroyer. And since statistics provided an intellectual method of rationalizing what happened in time, the changing no longer had to be relegated to a realm of mere appearance.

It was not astonishing, therefore, that new principles of valuation were gradually announced. One began to hear of *powerfulness*, of *growth*, of the *dramatic*, of *contrast*, of the *emotional*, of the *vital*, as terms of praise. Evenness of tone became monotony, mechanical balance became lifeless, and in the twentieth century, by an extraordinarily logical development of this non-logical process, artists were urged to lay aside all instruction and to let their inner natures, which in practice meant whatever came into their heads, take its place. The works of art made by the naive, the childlike, the primitive, were found to have desirable qualities which academic works of art lacked, and they were, not unnaturally, those qualities which could not be attained through instruction. A child's painting might not be very accurate as representation, even when it set out to represent something, but it was fresh, spontaneous, innocent. In the case of the Sunday-painters, their works might lack that balanced composition which was admired in the canvases of Raphael, Poussin, and Ingres, but they had a poignancy of expression and dramatic intensity which Raphael, Poussin and Ingres would have thought vulgar. The drawings and carvings of primitive people lacked the perfection and grace of the Apollo Belvedere, but they had a freedom from tradition—by which was meant the European tradition—which was refreshingly vital.

But when one sat down to reflect on all this, it could be seen that just as static form had to be perceived in matter and therefore was inevitably going to be compensated by elements of the dynamic, so dynamic form would be found in matter and would be compensated by the static. Both kinds of form are found in everything, even in the song of a bird or the web of a spider. The problem was that of accommodating the form of a temporal art, like that of music, to the form of a spatial art, like that of painting. In the one case, where the spatial forms became the paradigm, music was considered as if it were spread out in two dimensions; in the other, where temporal forms were the paradigm, painting was considered in its dynamic aspects and compared to music.

One can see the two approaches if one thinks about a play, for a play takes time and, being a situation, can be seen as a whole.

Let us conclude this discussion then by indicating this in *King Lear.*

From the point of view of static form, one perceives two fathers, each with good and bad children: Lear with Regan and Goneril balanced by Cordelia; Gloucester with his evil bastard son, Edmund, balanced by his good legitimate son, Edgar. Both were duped by their bad children and hence unjust to their good. But the two sets of evil children are also balanced: Regan and Goneril being in love with Edmund, their jealousy of each other leading to their undoing; Edmund's treachery to his father and half-brother leading to his, when he is denounced by Albany, the husband of Goneril, and killed by Edgar, the brother whom he has wronged. The two good children are not quite so evenly balanced; for though Cordelia is killed through an act of Edmund's, thus punishing her father, Edgar does not suffer except through the death of his father. In the case of the two fathers, Lear is punished not only by his evil children, to whom he has attempted to do good, but also by the death of his good child; Gloucester is blinded.[10]

But this mechanical balance is presented of course in a series of acts, as plays must be, and hence there is a certain dynamic form accompanying it. Thus the first two scenes of Act I, are a presentation of the fathers' fatuity. From

[10] In the prototype of this play, *The Chronicle History of King Leir,* the play ends happily with Lear restored to his throne. His death in Shakespeare's play is the weakest part of the structure, being attributable at most to his poor judgment in having sought refuge with a French rather than an English army. But he had little choice in the matter. But see Snider's criticism as cited in the Variorum ed.

Act I, scene iii to Act III, there is a growing revelation of the daughters' treachery over against Edmund's treachery. The climax would appear to come in Act III, in Lear's abandonment in the tempest and Gloucester's blindness. Act IV begins the dénouement, as Albany begins to suspect his wife's villainy, and step by step all evil is unmasked. Act V brings the finale in the death of Lear.

It would be false to assert that either kind of form is the more important in this—or any other—play. If *King Lear* has any one form at all, it is the compound of the two, one played against the other. And this, we surmise, will be true of any work of art whatsoever in which a design can be discovered. Some, as we have said above, will tend towards the static more than towards the dynamic, others in the opposite direction. Our conclusion is that each is a metaphor which cannot be exhaustively used and thus requires supplementation from the other.

CHAPTER SIX

ART AND NATURE

1. *Thesis*

THE STATE of psychology is such that in this section of our study we can do little more than venture an hypothesis which may turn out to be false, but which appears at the present time to be justified. It is the thesis that the habits acquired through the various arts of perceiving things in a certain pattern are transferred to everyday perception and thus help to determine the objective character of the world. If this thesis is true, we can see the reason for maintaining that we see through the eyes of the artist and the notion that art imitates nature demands correction even in the representative arts.

2. *Perception is selective*

Though common-sense may maintain that our sense-organs are transparent glasses through which we see the world as it is, no one with the slightest knowledge of science can take so simple a point of view. There are a few obstacles to so gratifying a belief of which we choose one or two as examples.

Human beings are primarily visual and mobile animals. Our world is essentially a world of shapes, colors, and moving objects. When we pass beyond vision, our vocabulary is poverty stricken, our color adjectives being numerous and discriminatory, our olfactory adjectives being few and synoptic. To name a smell or a taste, or for that matter a sound, is very difficult for most of us, such experiences do not have names. If we could put ourselves in the position of dogs, who, one imagines, are predominantly olfactory, it is clear that our perceptions would be very different from those which we actually enjoy. Dogs will overlook visual data, which are clear and compulsive to us, to pursue odors which we do not perceive; they hear sounds which are inaudible to us, a fact which permitted the Army to develop a whistle to call dogs whch no human ear could hear. The human equation enters into every perceptual statement which we make about the external world and if we imagine that we can develop an art which will eliminate it, we are seriously deceived.

Thus in the epistemologies of what Reid called the Cartesian tradition, physical objects are supposed to have a certain location in space determined by their physical properties. They are objects which do not extend beyond that area of space at which one touches them. If one define the objective frontier tactually, it is clear that contradictions arise when we try to locate the visual, the auditory, the olfactory, objects in that same place. For the visual frontier is where one sees the object, the place at which it becomes visible; the auditory frontier the place at which it becomes audible; the olfactory frontier the place at which it becomes odorous. But one can see things which are inaudible, an experience which every child has had who has seen the steam come out of a locomotive's whistle before he hears it. One smells things which are inaudible—flowers. One hears things where one cannot smell them. The tactile and gustatory frontiers of an object are closest, since contact is required to perceive textures and tastes; there follow in order probably the olfactory, the auditory, and the visual. Moreover the volumes of each of these objects varies, being sometimes sharply defined, at other times vague. By convention we can call the visual-tactile object the real object, if we wish, and indeed in most literature and painting we have become used to reality described in such terms. But we know upon a moment's reflection that such practice is simply human practice and that if we wished to take a superhuman point of view, no kind of perceptual object would be any realer than another.

I am not arguing that one should adopt the point of view of either angels or animals, for we cannot. We must construct intellectually a world which fits human needs; otherwise we could not orient ourselves in it. But at the same time when we are talking about the relation between nature and art, we had best be clear about the problem involved in the situation. The perceptual object, then, is first of all selected out of the possible range of perceptions by the general limitations of the human perceptual apparatus. One can corroborate this by reading the usual descriptive passages in novels or poems.

But besides the human equation, there is the personal equation. We are not referring here to the technical meaning of this term in astronomical observations, but to individual differences in perception. One man's powers of observation just happen to be different from another's. One man is endowed at birth or by training with a greater gift of discrimination, sees what others do not see, has sharper powers of taste or smell or hearing. If a dog can hear sounds too highly pitched for human ears, so one man distinguishes timbres to which another is deaf. It is futile to ask which is right, for both are. Perception is in part a function of the perceptual equipment of human beings; in part to be sure a function of the objective stimulus, the light rays, air waves, or chemical composition.

If training has any effect on what a person perceives, we can legitimately ask what directs his attention. One sees or does not see in part what one is looking for or has been taught to look for.[1] It is questionable whether, as far as perception can be distinguished from sensation, one would perceive anything if one were not first interested in finding out whether it was there. There is, of course, an objective field of stimuli whose existence it would be folly to deny. But within that enormous field, there is a selection going on of possible sensations and perceptions which requires some guiding principle before it becomes operative. Whether we see a rose or an example of the variety, *Ami Quinard,* is not exclusively determined by what is before us. One has to know prior to the observation that there is such a variety of rose, what it looks like, its color, shape, petal structure, leaf formation, odor, texture, and so on. But to make that observation depends upon a good deal of previous knowledge of roses, knowledge which may have been picked up in a seedman's catalogue. If one is now asked to describe an *Ami Quinard,* it is not inevitable that one describe it in terms of color and odor; one may describe it in botanical terms. Thus the *Encyclopedia Britannica* (11th edition) under *Rose* says, "In most cases the rose of the poets and the rose of the botanist are one and the same in kind, but popular usage has attached the name rose to a variety of plants whose kinship to the true plant no botanist would for a moment admit." Continuing to say that only the botanical meaning of the word will be used, the article states, "They (roses) are erect or climbing shrubs, never herbs or trees, generally more or less copiously provided with straight or hooked prickles of

---

[1] See Jerome S. Bruner and Leo Postman; "Symbolic Value as an Organizing Factor in Perception," *Journal of Social Psychology,* (1948) XXVII, pp. 203-208.

various shapes and glandular hairs. . . . The leaves are invariably alternate, provided with stipules, and unequally pinnate, the leaflets varying in number from one . . . to 11 or even 15, the odd leaflet always being at the apex, the others in pairs. . . ." Though there is nothing here, nor in the rest of the article, which contradicts ordinary sensory perception, it is doubtful that the average observer of roses ever sees all this. Were he trained in botany, he would, and moreover would see it before he noticed any of the more sensuous traits of the flower. On the other hand, a catalogue of roses describes *Ami Quinard* as follows: " Semi-double, fragrant, black lustered red. The petals are like two-toned velvet, deep crimson to velvety black, depending on how the light strikes the curve of the petals. Move the flower and the play of black and crimson shifts and changes with it. Buds deep maroon, urn shaped, ideal for boutonnières." And adds, need it be said, the price.

Clearly no one would ask, thinking he was asking an intelligent question, which of these is the real rose, which the true description, which closest to the facts.[2] There are, it is undeniable, a very great number of things which one can say about a rose, things which one can observe, and it should be obvious that which of these one is going to observe depends upon the context of one's thoughts, not upon one's sense-organs. The context is determined by the whole net-work of relations into which the observable facts

---

[2] It is not without interest that the first quotation which Littré gives under the word *rose* says nothing about its color or shape, but plays upon the brevity of its life. It is the much quoted,

> Mais elle était du monde où les plus belles choses
> Ont le pire destin,
> Et rose elle a vécu ce que vivent les roses,
> L'espace d'un matin . . .

are to be integrated, so that the *mot juste* derives its appropriateness not simply from the sensory data before one, but also from what one is going to do with these data. One's attention demands orientation. The orientation is relevant to one's interests, pragmatic, intellectual, sentimental, call them what you will. But again, it should be repeated, this is not inconsistent with the belief that there is a physical object before one.

3. *The determination of the selective principle*

It is probable that most descriptions will be largely visual in language. That is determined by the human equation. But this does not mean that visual descriptions are the uniquely proper descriptions, the descriptions which have a prior right to be called factual. Being the kind of creatures that we are, we find visual descriptions more useful than auditory or olfactory descriptions. A description of human experience in physiological terms or in terms of physics or chemistry would be just as factual. They would also be more shocking to our feelings. We are accustomed to using the adjective " real " for the world as described by physics, first by Galilean physics, in which the real world was composed of things describable in terms which later became Locke's primary qualities, then by the physics of the molecules, then by that of the atoms, and finally by that of the sub-atomic world. When Eddington speaks of the real table as being largely empty space, he is not dealing with any table which our senses can observe; on the contrary, his table is derived ultimately from our sensory observations, to be sure, but they are controlled and disciplined by various techniques of measurement so that their sensory origin is completely lost. Facts, it may be said are predetermined by the total complex of ideas into which they are to be integrated, whether we are aware of what that complex is or not. It was a fact for Aristotle that heavy objects fell faster than light ones; for Galileo it was a fact that they all fell with the same acceleration. But Aristotle was thinking of objects as they fell through some such medium as air or water; for Galileo they were falling in a vacuum.[3]

There is, we are insisting, a ritual of observation at work here of which we do not have to be conscious at every moment of our lives, but which is operative whether we are aware of it or not. It operates very much as the rules of language operate, absorbed into our habits and thus more or less compulsory. When an elementary book on rhetoric defines description as "that form of writing whose purpose is to suggest a picture," its author is following a tradition which has served its purpose well, even if truer to nineteenth century practice than to earlier. When it goes on to say, " It seeks in the main to portray the outside world as it is revealed to us by means of our five senses," the catch lies in the words, " in the main," for the author knows enough of history to be aware of the descriptive methods of older writers and also knows that there is no point in confusing the minds of high-school students with epistemological problems and cultural history. There was a time when sensory descriptions did not have the vogue which they have had since the Romantic Movement vivified experience. The fact that French poetry of the seventeenth century was less given to descriptions of " Nature " than English poetry, is surely not to be explained by the defective eyesight of the French, but rather to their acceptance of a literary tradition different from

---

[3] Students of epistemology and scientific method will pardon the superficiality of this statement. We have made only those points which are relevant to aesthetics.

that which prevailed in England. In fact, French poetry
of the sixteenth century is full of descriptive passages.

The cultural determination of the selective principle
becomes even clearer when we observe what different
people of different times having seen in a given work of
art.[4] We have said above that Shylock has been re-
interpreted since Shakespeare's day when he was in all
probability a comic figure. He has in fact gone through
at least five different stages. If we ask which of these is
the correct interpretation and if we mean by " correct "
that which would have been acceptable to Shakespeare,
then it is likely that Burbadge's interpretation is correct.
But then the question arises why the interpretation should
have changed. The answer must surely lie in the change
in our ideas about Jews. Few people in Shakespeare's
time would have seen the Jewish community as an " unfortunate nation " as Kean did (1814) ; the Jews had been
forbidden to enter England as early as 1290 and it was not

[4] Bruner and Postman in the article cited above demonstrate how
their subjects actually magnified the size of certain objects which
they were looking at because of cultural determinations. In their
own words (*Op. cit.*, p. 206) , " *Value*, whether positive or negative,
leads to perceptual accentuation. . . . Apparently, that which is
' important ' to the subject looms larger in perception. . . . " And
again, (p. 207) " That which is desired or fulfills a need tends to be
emphasized in perception through magnification. The organism, as it
were, maximizes the reward value of the object. When a negative
symbol is of such a nature as to alert the organism to danger or
threat, it is reasonable to suppose that positive accentuation may
also occur. In terms of the adaptive functions of perception, accentuation of negative symbols may aid under certain conditions in preparing the organism for defense and action. . . . Value, then, whether
positive or negative, is a determinant of subjective size. . . ." In
plain English this means that when a person sees the symbol of something which he either likes or dislikes, a dollar-sign, the Nazi swastika,
the Christian cross, he will see it larger than life-size.

until the visit of Menasseh ben Israel to Cromwell in 1655 that the possibility of their return was legalized. The Jew could be as much of a comic figure in 1596 as a Negro could be in America in 1896. " Unfortunate nations," are a modern invention, that is, a nineteenth century invention. One would have about as much reason to read into the text of the *Merchant of Venice* Kean's interpretation as one would to read back into it the interpretation of Brown (1838) that it was a plea for toleration or that of Kreyssig (1862) that it was a plea for prudence. But the comic Shylock has seemed so forbidding to some actors and producers that they have actually cut passages out of the text to make their interpretation appear more authentic.

This is but one example. One can think of many others. One remembers how Zola made the characters of men and women in his Rougon-Macquart series fit a preconceived theory of heredity. For him a character was not a capricious compound of sense, will, and reason, but the effect of certain genetic laws over which he had no control. What went into the novels was determined not by surface observation of men and women, but by the science of biology as Zola knew it through Claude Bernard. Or one can recall how the pseudo-science of phrenology or that of physiognomonics affected what people saw in other people's faces: the determined jaw, the sensual mouth, the wild eyes, the ascetic lips, the ambitious nose, the philosophical brow. . . . Descriptions of characters in nineteenth century novels to a large part were conditioned by what their authors knew at first or second hand of writers like Lavater, Gall, or Spurzheim. One can see a chin, but one cannot see the ambition in a chin; that requires interpretation. But perhaps one of the most eloquent examples of the transformation of perceptual objects through cultural determinants is to be found in the following quotation cited by Ogden, Richards, and Wood in their *Foundations of Aesthetics*.

We demand that a painter should choose for his theme beautifully shaped objects, such as human figures, male or female, in graceful attitudes, nude and exquisitely formed, with rounded limbs, or clothed in flowing drapery, Greek or Roman, Oriental or Florentine; animals like the fawn, the panther, the Arab charger, the swan, and the butterfly; mountain peaks, bossy hills, winding bays; the cataract leaping in an arch from the crag; Naples and Vesuvius and Niagara, the curved horizon of ocean, the thousand inlets of a highland loch; graceful pottery, elegantly moulded goblets, flagons, and vases, slender beakers and shapely chalices; the domes and minarets of Stamboul, the sweeping arches of Tintern and Poitiers, the columns of Paestum, the rounded tiers and galleries of the amphitheatre. On the other hand, the painter generally avoids (except for some special effect of colour or contrast) lean, harsh, and angular limbs or features, constrained and graceless clothing, awkward postures and action; heavy, ungainly, or shapeless animal forms, such as the bear, the cart-horse, the goose, and the slug; flat, monotonous plains; the still ocean unbroken by a winding shore or bluff headland, unrelieved by a ship with bellied sails or a tempest curling the breakers on the beach; straight streets, plain rectangular houses, square windows, and flat façades destitute of arch or column, dome or portico.[5]

If ever there was a paragraph in which the words " the painter " were equivalent to " those painters of whom I approve," it is this one. Not only are the appropriate objects of painting not those which are found in Chinese and Japanese painting, but not even those found in the major works of European painting. All Byzantine painting is excluded, most of the Italian painting before Raphael, all of El Greco, much of Goya,[6] a good deal of Dutch and Flemish painting, and all painting stemming from Courbet and Cézanne. In fact, Allen exhibited the limitations of

[5] Grant Allen, *Physiological Aesthetics*, p. 233.
[6] Cf. the illustrations in Ogden-Richards-Wood, *op. cit.*

his taste as those of the Royal Academy in the middle and late Victorian period.

4. *The affective coefficient*

But it will be noticed that Grant Allen in this paragraph not merely lists those objects which are fit to be painted, but also indicates that they are pleasing. In other words, he is not saying that the painter should select out of his environment certain objects, but that the objects selected are also beautiful in themselves. Whatever may be the explanation of our sense of beauty or of our views on the necessity of artists' depicting or creating beautiful things, it is clear that Grant Allen felt his nudes, his fawns, his slender beakers, and sweeping arches to be beautiful, and bears, geese, still oceans, straight streets, and flat façades to be ugly. Since there have been a great number of human beings who have not felt this—witness Chinese painting of geese, Utrillo's straight streets, and Hobbema's avenue of trees,—the pleasantness or disagreeableness of the objects cannot be a function of them in isolation from humanity nor can it be said that all human beings feel the same way about them. Since the human race is biologically one, it must be concluded that the affective coefficient attached to objects is determined by the culture of the people who look at them. No one ever saw a Chinese painting made before the influx of Western customs into the Orient which included a nude. Are we to decide that the Chinese had a deficient sense of beauty or that they had a cultural tradition which made them regard clothed figures as more beautiful than naked figures ?

There is one generalization about humanity which one can make without fear of contradiction. It is that people like, dislike, approve and disapprove of things in their experience, even when those things are as simple as colors, tastes, sounds, textures, and odors. Much of our literature is given over to praising and blaming. From it one judges that the number of things which people like and dislike is about equal to the number of things which they have experienced. If fact, this is so true that ethicists such as the Stoics pleaded with their disciples to attain a kind of emotional neutrality towards the world in order to achieve that peace of mind characteristic of the Sage. The writer of these words has lived long enough to have listened to more lectures and to have read more books than he can remember, and it is with the greatest difficulty that he can recall a conversation about facts, conduct, works of art, or even ideas in which the protagonists did not feel it their duty to tell their *vis-à-vis* not merely what they were talking about, but also whether they liked it or not. He has heard some lecturers, professors of literature, who felt a strong compulsion to tell their listeners that they would be remiss in their duty if they did not express their emotions about their subject.

Liking and approbation, disliking and disapprobation, form so large a part of aesthetics that they will be given separate treatment, but we may anticipate by saying that at their simplest they are rooted in judgment.

5. *Judgment and feeling*

Whether any experiences are pleasant or unpleasant in themselves is still a matter of dispute. Watson demonstrated at one time that babies find the sensation of being dropped and loud noises distasteful to them and presumably a baby is as close to the raw human being as one can get. This does not, however, mean that babies dislike making loud noises or dropping things, a distinction important to remember when reading back into the mind of the artist the feelings which his works of art inspire in a spectator. But aside from this rudimentary case of un-motivated feeling, it is impossible to find any expression of liking or disliking uncolored by social and cultural conditions. Even a baby is not allowed to experiment freely, eating, drinking, touching, smelling whatever he may be interested in. He grows up from a very early age in an atmosphere of prohibitions and encouragements. His nurse, his parents, his siblings, his school-mates, all join in approving and disapproving of him, rewarding and punishing him. One might say that at least approval by one's associates is in itself pleasant, but after all it takes so many forms that it is at best a vague verbal formula. If one assumes that it is accompanied by punishments and rewards which are painful and pleasant respectively, one observes also that some presumably painful experiences turn out to be sought by the child, as Freud pointed out many years ago only too clearly.

This all boils down to the fact that one cannot catch a human being out of social context and before the social system of rewards and punishments has done its preliminary work of training the child to satisfy his interests in an approved way and not to satisfy them in disapproved ways. Consequently, as soon as one can catch a human being, judgment has already entered into his valuations, not his own judgment necessarily, but at a minimum that of his mother or nurse. What he finds pleasant therefore is equivalent to what he has been taught to find pleasant, and what he finds unpleasant is equally a product of learning, not innate taste.

He thus transfers to the physical objects, potential sources of satisfaction, the approbation conferred by his environment, and the rest of his immaturity is spent in swinging between the satisfactions which he has learned are legitimate and those which he is learning are illegiti-

mate. For as soon as he can walk, he begins to associate
with new people and hence new sets of standards come into
play, a source of worry, sometimes a source of satisfaction,
to his parents. The judgments which determine that a
given manner of satisfying an interest is agreeable are
often forgotten. They have been absorbed into the child's
makeup and he seeks or avoids certain experiences with
no conscious motive at all. He simply *knows* that some
things are dirty and must be avoided, that some practices
are disgusting and must not be indulged in. Whatever
lingering fondness he may have for them will be repressed
and the image of them will be stuffed into his unconscious
and kept there as far as such repression is at all possible.
We have learned in the last fifty years that no experience
is entirely repressible and that even our most potent
taboos are violated cunningly enough to satisfy those who
wish to violate them without being caught. Thus the fact
that a judgment is concealed or automatic through habit
or compulsive and thus unquestioned is no evidence that
it has played no part in determining the affective coefficient of a given experience.

Such judgments may be moral, religious, social, aesthetic, what you will. The person who, reading Shylock's
words, spoken when he hears of Jessica's exchanging her
mother's ring for a monkey, " It was my turquoise; I had it
of Leah when I was a bachelor," and feels their pathos, is
not merely hearing the words, but reading into them a feeling which may be natural enough for him to experience
but which was probably not intended by Shakespeare at
all. We are likely to have a similar attitude towards the
famous lines of Lucretius (II, 1) which express sentiments
about the misfortunes of others repugnant to us but so
right and proper to Lucretius that he stated them as a
commonplace.

We cannot escape from some social context in which our values are fixed. Even when we withdraw from social commitments to the limits of our capacity for isolation, we are still at the mercy of our thoughts and dreams. And they have their origin in our associations. It may be right to practice the technique of rebellion at certain times and we are not preaching submission to all the demands which are made upon us. But let us not deceive ourselves into thinking that we have achieved complete independence of thought. At the very least, the symbols which we use and which in part determine what we shall think are not our own. In fact, the very impulse which drives us towards isolation springs from the social complex. We shall approve of certain things and acts which a good part of society does not approve of, but what we shall seek for ourselves will be determined in reaction to the very ideals which we are trying to avoid. Isolation is the denial of society; it is nothing but a zero in itself; and, if we are to do anything in our cave or wine-jar, it will probably be penance for the things which we have done in society. We are not the first to point out that one cannot escape the past except through death.

6. *The transformation of the object*

Thus natural objects will become symbols of approved and disapproved ideas. The landscape will be a fresco of hieroglyphs and the sermons in stones, the singing of brooks, the laughter of April, and all the other rigamarole of those who invest geography with human traits will be dragged out and paraded before the eye. So beakers will become graceful, cataracts will leap, arches will sweep, and a cart-horse become ungainly. Some things, like parts of the human body, will become downright obscene, ugly, profane; others will become beautiful and uplifting, sacred, edifying. When mountains stopped being ominous in the second half of the eighteenth century, when woman became enigmatic at the beginning of the nineteenth, when workingmen ceased being comic in the middle of the nineteenth, the changes were attributable not to any change in the physical aspects of the things in question but to our attitude towards them. That attitude in turn was determined by changes in the complex of ideas which was absorbed as correct by the dominant class in society.

One of the sources of this sort of change lay in the movement known as naturalism. Naturalism laid it down as a cardinal principle that whatever an artist's eye saw was worth recording. The artist, whether painter or writer, turned into a recorder. Thus Courbet could say, *Le beau, c'est le laid*. His famous *Stone-crushers* was one of his first contributions to an art which rested upon this principle. But his opponents could see in this picture an argument for socialism. Yet Courbet to our eyes was not presenting an argument for anything. He was simply painting a picture of two stone-crushers at work. Why this subject-matter should have been thought of as propaganda for a social philosophy can be understood only if one think of the great tradition in criticism, which maintained that only noble personages could enact tragedies, that lowly folk were in essence comic. When Bellori attacked Caravaggio, it was on the ground that he used common people to represent the Blessed Virgin and the other characters of biblical legend. He was " too naturalistic." [7] One has but to read the works of the Renaissance followers of Aristotle and Horace to see why this should have become hardened into a ritual. The nobility was noble, the commoners were

---

[7] See E. G. Holt, *op. cit.*, p. 321. Footnote 3, on the same page, gives a classical explanation for anti-naturalism.

common, and the concealed puns in the two adjectives were taken seriously. In the second place, work was a penance for the sin of Adam and it was not until the nineteenth century that anyone of influence preached the doctrine of the dignity of labor. In the third place, if the artist was to seek the universal, he must turn away from the " natural," since natural objects were always particulars. In the fourth place, socialists did draw common people. Daumier, in order to ridicule classicism (idealism) out of existence, caricatured the ancient myths and he drew the nude body as it actually appeared in the baths. Since Daumier was a well-known opponent of the Bourgeois Monarchy and also drew poor laundresses, travelers in third class carriages, street singers, and all this seriously, he must have been a socialist. For all these and other reasons, the depiction of the two stone-crushers at work was politically revolutionary, and, what is more to the point, ugly.[8]

It is our thesis that we transform the object by either unconscious or conscious judgments, which entail judgments of value. These affect what we perceive, not only by selecting some features and neglecting others, but by actually modifying their quality. But since some of these judgments come to us from the arts, we may be said to see the world through the eyes of the artist.

---

[8] On Daumier, see *Il faut être de son temps* Appendix I. On Courbet, see *Courbet and the Naturalistic Movement, passim.*

CHAPTER SEVEN

APPROBATION AND LIKING

1. *Definitions*

ONE OF THE complications of a theory of aesthetics is that we do not stand in emotional neutrality before works of art and processes of artistry, like biologists before protozoa or chemists before their white precipitates, but on the contrary are emotionally involved with almost every aesthetic object which we study. There may be some pictures, poems, musical compositions, and buildings which leave us totally unmoved, but in general, it is believed, we are either pleasantly or unpleasantly affected by them all. In fact, much of the writing known as criticism consists of putting into words either our love or our hate for a given work of art or kind of artistry, or what we imagine to be the reasons for our love or hate. We should like to distinguish in this chapter two attitudes which are entailed in this matter; we shall call them liking and disliking, approbation and disapprobation.

(a) *Liking.* By liking we shall mean our response to those things which seem to be inherently agreeable. When a desire is satisfied, whether it be hunger, thirst, lust, aggressiveness, friendliness, or any other of those interests which seem primitive, we are pleased; when the same desires are frustrated, we are displeased. No one who is hungry and eats has to worry about whether the food he is eating is precisely what would be best for his system,

117

whether the requisite number of calories is present in it or not, whether something else would not be more appropriate to the occasion. The drive demands satisfaction and one's critical faculties are stilled. One is in the condition of a dog who has been without food for some time and who throws himself wildly upon the object which will fill the abyss in his belly. Most civilized people in the United States have never been in such a state of imperious longing for food, but everyone has experienced in some field of desire equally compulsive drives which can be substituted for the example given.

There seem to be certain objects in the range of aesthetics which are similarly agreeable, certain pieces of music which are pleasant even to ears innocent of musical knowledge, pictures which people just like or dislike without having the faintest idea of why they like or dislike them. The success of popular music, the pictures on the covers of popular magazines, the kind of poetry which is printed on Christmas cards, the kind of domestic architecture which is exemplified by the thousands in the suburbs to our cities, are all specimens of works of art which do not appear to require any justification. It would be absurd to argue that the partisans of such works of art study them first to see whether they live up to certain standards and then decide to like them. A man who dreams of a popular movie star does not first compare her measurements to those of the Venus de Milo and then decide deliberately and after mature reflection to dream of her. Men do not agree, to be sure, on which particular star is the optima companion of their dreams, but whoever she may be, she is chosen without hesitation by the stirring of one's bowels. So there used to be adolescents who pinned on their walls reproductions of the ladies painted by Rossetti, just as now, I suppose, their analogues of 1949 pin up photographs of the paintings of Picasso. Choices of this sort seem to be made spontaneously, as the result of what has been— badly—called instinctive taste. For there seems to be a folk-belief that taste is automatic, direct, and without thought. Taste can obviously become automatic through habit, and we know that acquired tastes can be just as compulsive as tastes which arise in infancy. Witness the taste for alcohol and tobacco.

Liking, then, we shall say has sunk to the level below reflection. This will satisfy those readers who wish it to be non-intellectual and at the same time will satisfy the more scientifically minded who will wish it to be less mysterious than it sometimes is.

(b) *Approbation.* Approbation, on the contrary, is always above the level of reflection, as we use the term. Approbation arises when we observe in an object or act the exemplification of certain principle, certain rules, certain standards. Thus one approves of good English and means by good English that speech which exemplifies and conforms to the rules of grammar, syntax, and rhetoric. One approves of good behaviour, and can point to its exemplification of the principles of courtesy, politeness, correct etiquette. One approves of a sonnet and points out how the sonnet conforms to the rules of correct sonnet-writing. One approves of a fugue because it is written in strict obedience to the rules laid down in the text-books on fugal composition. Works or art and acts which obey the rules are correct, like the answers to arithmetical problems and could, I suppose, be turned out on a machine, as indeed many of them have been.

It is clear that one need not like that of which one approves, nor dislike that of which one disapproves. Indeed one is usually in the position of liking that of which one disapproves and disliking that of which one approves. Our problem in ethics or in aesthetics is to bring the two into harmony with each other. The words which Ovid puts into the mouth of Medea, *Video meliora proboque, deteriora sequor,* have ceased to be a quotation and have turned into a proverb, so common is the circumstance which they describe. Though they applied originally to a matter of conduct, they apply equally well to works of art. And in fact it is not uncommon to hear critics depreciating some works of art because they are too correct. The adverb, *too,* usually seems to indicate the critic's dislike, not disapprobation, of correctness. To be too faultless sounds like an impossibility, like *too square* or *too circular.* One could not imagine a correct answer to an arithmetical problem being too correct. Does not the apparent impossibility point to an essential element in aesthetic appreciation: our desire to feel a balance between spontaneity and mechanism, between freedom and determinism?

2. *The conditions of liking*

Such questions could be answered more easily, were the psychology of our affective life better understood. We believe that hunger and sexuality, which might be called basic biological drives, whether they are approved of or not, demand satisfaction and that their satisfaction is liked regardless of whether it is approved of or not. The satisfaction of hunger in the circles which are likely to read this book presents no serious problem until it reaches the level of piggishness. Sexuality, however, is still a question of debate and there are more ways of satisfying our lusts which are disapproved than ways which are approved. Yet a man will find a means of satisfying his sexuality, regardless of what society may say, even if he has to lie to himself about it. And it is scarcely probable that such devious ways would be pursued unless the persons in question found a deep satisfaction in them. A person who has reached the age of maturity knows that the harshest legal penalties have not prevented mankind from doing what he wants to do; they have merely taught him the art of hypocrisy, disguise, and concealment.

For as soon as one emerges from the cradle, one is peppered with prohibitions. And it is safe to say that although no society could have survived which utterly forbade the satisfaction of either hunger and sexuality, none has existed which has not attempted to control them.

Though an interest may be inherent in the biological man, the ways of satisfying it are determined culturally. Social approbation, not necessarily of society as a whole, for no one lives in all of any society, will bring prestige and prestige may demand the most rigorous denial of our basic needs. No society ever demanded that men starve to death as a general rule; but every society has laid down rules for what one can eat decently, when one can eat, how one may eat, how much one may eat, the order of eating, whom one may eat with. Attempts to demonstrate the appropriateness of such taboos and regulations to social survival have all failed. One tribe of Indians eats mussels, a neighboring tribe refuses to eat them. One social group eats three meals a day, another eats four or five. In one nation men and women eat together, in another they eat apart. Hindus will eat no meat, but will eat vegetables; Moslems will eat meat with the exception of pork, and both live in the same climate and country and survive to the same degree.[1] There exists at present no special material cause of such taboos, whatever may have been their origin. The reason for them is tradition, sometimes backed

[1] Cf. Saint Jerome on food-taboos, in *Adversus Jovianum*, II, vii, for an early European example of curiosity about all this.

by religion. Such reason is no less compulsive than material necessity or other external forces and probably accounts in large measure for the repulsion which people find in violating their society's taboos. Prestige in the form of social approbation is at stake.

Let us mention among the many other culturally determined interests only two: the desire for power and the desire for understanding. It is not true that in every society individuals want power over others or that in those societies in which power is highly regarded, it is achieved in the same way, directed towards the same people and things, and exercised through the same techniques. There have been, as Ruth Benedict pointed out, societies in which power was despised. But we also know without having recourse to technical works on anthropology, that the kind of power which is exercised in a gang, physical power, the power of actually and literally ruling over others through the fists, similar to the kind of power which the Big Nations now exert over the little, is believed by members of other societies to be inferior to the kind of power which a man like Gandhi possessed, and which is sometimes called moral power. Thousands of people did what Gandhi told them to do and did it without question. Gandhi moreover had no power of excommunication, no magical technique of shutting men out of heaven, or even of hurting their bodies here on earth, but nevertheless he had only to issue an order for great masses of people to obey. We may, if we wish, call the power of Gandhi and that of an Al Capone both by the same name, for both men had the ability to induce others to obey their commands. But after all the differences are greater than the similarities. Consequently, if we conclude from these two instances that the followers of both men liked obedience to

power, we are arguing more on the evidence of a pun than
on that of fact.

Similar remarks might be made about the desire for
understanding. I suppose that no people has ever existed
which preferred ignorance to knowledge, though occasion-
ally writers have published works which seemed in harmony with such a preference. But the techniques of ac-
quiring knowledge run from the Mystic Way to that of the
laboratory; some men believe in the authority of the
written word, others in the necessity of individual investi-
gation; some men think that everything is open to human
scrutiny, others that some subjects should be kept secret;
some think that all men should try to know all things,
others that a selected few should have access to the truth;
some think that everything worth knowing has already
been discovered, others that there are still boundless fields
of science to be explored. What can be known, what
should be known, who is to know it, how it can and should
be studied, are questions still fiercely debated by educa-
tionalists who agree on the vague words, " the desirability
of knowledge," so long as they are kept sufficiently vague.
Our conclusion is that we may like and dislike not merely
the satisfaction of those interests which might be considered basic, but also those which are culturally determined. For few of us know that the latter are not also
basic.

But not only is this so, it is also true that the culturally
determined interests may modify the basic interests.
Prestige may demand the flat denial of certain basic drives.
In the monastic communities the members took oaths not
simply of obedience, but also of chastity and poverty.
They also practised self-mortification in the various forms
of asceticism. Whatever one may think of the desire to
command and to indulge one's desire for food and drink

and warmth, no one who knows the literature can maintain that the monks had an easy time of keeping their vow of chastity. (In fact, if they had, there would have been little merit in it.) But the high praise given to virginity rings clearly through Christian literature. Here is an indubitable example of the fact that human beings can desire the denial of one of their basic drives. No Christian believes that since the Fall man has been naturally chaste; chastity is recognized as a state attained through self-discipline against the demands of the flesh. And every Christian would argue that on that account alone it is desirable.

Similarly the desire for power and understanding may entail the denial of other interests. We thus learn to approve of certain satisfactions which are irreconcilable with basic drives. The process may easily cause a genuine and deeply felt dislike of the basic drives. The scholar who prefers his studies to family life and strongly dislikes as well as disapproves of wives and children, whatever escapades he may indulge in from time to time, probably despises himself for his escapades. For one can develop a sense of sin in regard to things which one's fellows see no harm in whatsoever. A literary or a scientific conscience can be as strong as a moral conscience, and nothing more is needed to explain their force than the demands of the social group of writers or scientists with which a man identifies himself.

All cultures probably organize the satisfaction of most human desires, whether basic or not. Business ethics, scientific methods, aesthetic practices, religious rituals, musical fashions, decency and indecency in costume, polite speech, are but a few instances of such controls in our own society. If there could exist hermits, people who suddenly materialized on uninhabited islands and survived, it is possible that they would have none of our inhibitions regarding the satisfaction of either their desire for food or sexual satisfaction. One has only to observe children, though they are controlled and disciplined from birth, to see that their standards are those of the higher animals. They will put anything into their mouths and as for their sexual cravings, the less said the better. Approbation and disapprobation, whatever may be true of liking and disliking, are social in origin. A child would consider any desire self justified.

3. *The interaction between liking and approbation*

It is obviously impossible to find a human being who has not been subject to social control. What such a human being would like or dislike is beyond discovery. Our problem is that of civilized people whose first awareness is that of other civilized people. As one grows, one soon becomes conscious of the hard fact that what one likes is seldom approved of by the powers in whose hands lies our destiny. Our parents, our nurses, our siblings, our teachers in school—for all teachers are not in schools, our friends and other associates, the merchants with whom we deal, the books and magazines we read, the radio speakers whom we listen to, the movies which we see, all spend a good bit of their time telling us that what we want to do is wrong, disgraceful, dishonest, dirty, ugly, commonplace, infantile, bestial, stupid, abnormal, illegal, immoral, or simply bad. Since in earlier years we can be prevented from doing some of the things thus qualified, and punished for doing others, we emerge out of our homes with a pretty firm set of rules and standards with which to criticise ourselves and others. We discover conflict between our likings and other people's approbations, between our dislikings and other people's disapprobations. Our problem becomes that of reconciling what we like and that of which we approve.

This may arise in a variety of ways. If we live provincial lives in a community of which we belong to the dominant class, going to the approved school, church, shops, wearing the approved clothes, and frequenting the approved social set, having enough money to stay in the dominant group or earning our living in the approved way, and if we never stray out of that community and never read magazines or newspapers written elsewhere and by some miracle never listen to the radio, there will be little likelihood of conflict. We shall know instinctively, as we wrongly say, what we ought to do and we shall like doing it. We shall have forgotten our early training and shall imagine that we have always done the right thing.

There is also the possibility that the kinds of things which are in keeping with the standards of our group are the kind of thing which we happen to like because of our original endowment. There are no doubt people who simply enjoy the exercise of power, for even in highly ritualized primitive societies there are peripheral types who are offenders, so that we must conclude that social approbation will never be sufficient to make every man enjoy doing what it prescribes. The man in some American communities who enjoys making money, being one of the boys, never admitting to having an abstract idea, despising professors, preferring engineers and doctors to literary historians and philosophers, in short the type which Mr. Sinclair Lewis has won fame by creating, will certainly find no difficulty in fitting into the pattern of culture of many small American towns. There are also some people who become aesthetic Bohemians, not out of piety to the memory of Verlaine, but because such a life is that best adapted to their natures. There are perhaps some " instinctive " radicals and some " instinctive " conservatives.

There is also the possibility of a person's admiration for another person being transferred to that person's standards. Most of us have been through the process of accepting without question the ideals of some older person, usually not a member of our family, and of attempting to realize them in our conduct. One has only to think of the emphasis which advertising puts on this sort of thing; of how the popular book reviews are little more than a statement of what the reviewer likes or dislikes, as if his feelings towards the book in question would of course be taken over by his readers; of the social pressure which the older boys in a school exert simply by existing.

There is in the fourth place the possibility of rationalizing our likings and dislikings and substituting for their psychological causes moral and aesthetic principles. We have learned enough about the process of rationalization in recent years to have become a bit distrustful of the reasons which people give for their preferences. But it should not be forgotten that the rationalizer has a wide choice of principles upon which to base his rationalizations. One of the problems which should arise is why he makes the particular choice he does make. When a man who belongs to a minority group comes out strongly for minority rights, one feels with some justification that he is not entirely objective or disinterested. But there is nevertheless a variety of reasons which can be brought forward to substantiate such rights, running from the principle of the brotherhood of man and the equality of all before the eyes of God, to the theory of natural rights. Sometimes, moreover, people who believe in these and similar principles do not believe in minority rights. Witness Jefferson who certainly believed in natural rights and also believed in the

intrinsic inferiority of the Negro and the legitimacy of
holding slaves. The choice of principles then is a problem
which we are unable to solve.

4. *The impossibility of an aesthetics built on basic needs*

Since no society permits the basic needs of an individual
to be satisfied without supervision and control, it is futile
to attempt to build an aesthetics on the analogy of the
" economic man." Such an economics was justified as an
eighteenth century scientific procedure, much as a theory
of dynamics based on the concept of bodies moving in free
space was justified. For science is said to depend on certain
primitive abstractions. But the weakness of such an economic theory lay in its inapplicability. There turned out to
be a conflict between the economic and the moral man at
certain times, in certain circumstances, or between the
economic and the aesthetic man, as when a person prefers
to do without a commodity because it does not satisfy his
sense of beauty; or between the economic and the religious
man, as when a person prefers poverty to ruthless economic
competition or mendacious advertising. The suspicion that
the data of psychology were not irrelevant to economics
created the " new economics " in the beginning of the
present century. It may not have had the logical purity
of the old, but turns out to be more verifiable. As one
imagined the economics of the economic man, so one could
imagine what an art would be like if there were a man
living in isolation and seeking exclusively the beautiful.
One could no doubt develop a set of theorems which
would be consistent and thus would have the formal elegance of geometry. But since our sense of beauty never
operates in isolation from our other senses, and since, even
if it could so operate, it would not be permitted to, there
is no possibility of working out an aesthetic theory ap-

plicable to man's aesthetic occupations on this basis. However much an individual might like certain things as aesthetic objects, he would learn to disapprove of them, though there is, to be sure, the chance that he might fortuitously and initially like those things of which society approves. It should be noted that we are not asserting the inevitable conflict between a man's original desires and socially approved ways of satisfying them; but we are indicating that most of the laws and customs of society were developed because of society's disapproval of such drives. No statute nor custom forbids people to eat or to procreate children; the laws and custom control the manner of eating and of procreation, and when a given manner becomes accepted by society as a whole, the law which once might have forbidden it, becomes obsolete.

5. *Approbation*

We shall not attempt to lay down fixed principles for approbation, for whatever principles one chooses turn out to have been preceded in history by others and the likelihood is that they too will change in time. But at present there is a tendency to base approbation on the following two sets of basic ideas: the importance of the interest satisfied and its harmony with other interests.

(a) *The importance of an interest has been judged in several ways.* (1) Sometimes one thinks of importance as that which is fundamental to the satisfaction of other interests. It is thus clear within certain limits that the desire for life—sometimes called the instinct of self-preservation—is basic if any interests at all are to be satisfied. The dead may be better off than the living, but here on earth it is clear that first of all one must be alive to enjoy anything whatsoever. One can think of no period in occidental society when it was generally agreed that any kind of existence was better than non-existence. On the contrary, it has usually been maintained that death is preferable to certain forms of life, though there has not always been general agreement on what forms of life were inferior to death. Consequently, even in the instance of this fundamental desire, the desire to go on living, one cannot be dogmatic and assert that its satisfaction is always approved. Otherwise, the man who leaps into the life-boat on a sinking ship, pushing women and children to the rear, as well as the man who flees before the enemy, would be the great heroes (or at any rate somewhat esteemed) of western society.

(2) A second meaning of "important" equates the important with that which is necessary for inherently better satisfactions. Thus one might maintain that to spend one's time in study was inherently better than to spend one's time making money, but nevertheless admit that unless one had a certain unearned income, or worked for one's living to earn a certain yearly wage, one could not enjoy the pleasures of study. Again, though there is no general agreement over the inherent value of bodily health, yet many people would maintain that it is prerequisite to the enjoyment of other values, such as the innocent pleasures of the athletic field, of social intercourse, or even walking in the country. To be a healthy animal, and nothing more, is usually deprecated by the stratum of society which reads books, but even the members of that stratum would admit that if one is an invalid, one's reading suffers.

(3) There is finally a hierarchy of values accepted by some thinkers, which will be mentioned in Chapter VIII, according to which some satisfactions are inherently lower

than others. " Importance " in this case would mean the
rank of a satisfaction within an accepted hierarchy. If
one believes that religious values are higher than all others,
one will approve of religious values, religious needs, religious acts, above all others, and no sacrifice will be considered to be too great for their satisfaction and practice.
No saint ever felt that his bodily needs had. any claim
whatever beyond the humiliation which they might inflict upon him, and many a religious person has refused the
claims of family, state, and community for the sake of his
religion. His position in this conflict does not rest upon
argument. No hierarchical arrangement of values could be
based upon prior argument, for the simple reason that the
hierarchy is in itself evidence of value, not a deduction
from anterior evidence. But of that, more later.

(b) The second of the usual bases for approbation is
the criterion of " harmony." It is maintained that a desire
is to be approved if it is in harmony with other desires,
does not militate against the achievement of other values,
increases the integration of our purposes. Almost any
interest if pursued beyond a certain point—which cannot be otherwise defined—will lead to conflict within ourselves or within the social groups whose purposes we have
adopted. There are traditional examples of this known to
everyone, such as the disapproval of over-working, over-
playing, self-indulgence, gluttony, debauchery, buffoonery,
or *anaesthesia,* to use an Aristotelian term. Clearly there
is no simple formula by which one can determine when one
has over-worked or over-indulged oneself or been a glutton,
a debauchee, or a buffoon. Temperance is one of those
mean conditions whose significance emerges after the act,
rather than before. One knows when one has drunk too
much; but one does not know ahead of time how much will

be too much, until one has had a great deal of experience.
And, as a matter of brute fact, one has a resistance to admitting that any amount is too much.

Moreover, the mean condition varies with different individuals and on different occasions. Is Dickens sentimental?
Is Browning over-optimistic? Is Rabelais obscene? [2]
Surely there are occasions when the excess does not appear and people to whom it does not appear. Even un-
reflective common-sense recognizes the legitimacy of obscenity on certain occasions and the legitimacy of prudery
on others. The harmony of values and desires can not be
decided *a priori*, for where harmony might exist in one
man's life or in one social situation, discord might arise
between the same desires or values in others. Adults usually recognize the fact that there is no necessary discord
between, for instance, the words of a song and the music,
while also recognizing that at times such a conflict might
arise. In our opinion the libretto of Purcell's *Dido and
Aeneas* is about as silly as even Nahum Tate at his silliest
could produce. But we can imagine the same music fitted
with reasonable words. There is, to take another example,
no necessary discord between our economic and our aesthetic interests, but frequently people admire the price of a

[2] I am omitting, for purposes of simplification, the consideration
that the words, Rabelais, Dickens, Browning, are the names of
writers not of specific passages in their works. Even if we believe
certain pages of Rabelais to be obscene, we have to admit that others
are not; and if we believe that the death of Little Nell is oversenti-
mental, we can hardly feel the same about the life of Sam Weller.
But such considerations introduce needless complications into an
argument already perhaps too complicated for ready comprehension.
The trouble arises probably from our habit of breaking our life up
into separate interests and considering their satisfactions in separation
also. Human life is a rope of many strands, not a collection of ex-
ternally related desires.

picture more than its beauty. The reader can extend this argument at his leisure.

The naive optimism which asserts that harmony is always possible must also be exploded. Human beings together with the societies they live in are too frequently in conflict, hoping perhaps for ultimate reconciliation but not counting on it. Sometimes these discords arise from ideals or from principles which are contradictory, as when a man's poverty leads to disease which leads to ignorance, or when the demands of the spirit are such that the demands of the flesh must be denied. Denial is not harmony, though it is a *modus vivendi*. The situation is analogous to that of the heroes of some tragedies: they are torn by equally compelling purposes and have to choose between them. Macbeth could scarcely satisfy his ambition—and that of his wife—while remaining faithful to his feudal lords; Antigone cannot obey both the law of the gods and that of the state. The choice which is rejection guides them both.

If this is so, it is hopeless to look for a form of art which will meet with the complete approval of all members of society and which will express the aims, or even the character, of society as an harmonious whole.

6. *Note on an apparent exception*

There is, however, no denying that any homogeneous society, or any group within a society, will assume the inherent value of its own self-preservation. That is, the preservation of the group, not of the individuals within it who may be called upon to die in order that the larger unit may live. There is no law of God which prevents social groups from dissolving when their purposes are accomplished. But it is to be observed that few do dissolve. The French nobility, for instance, has not renounced its titles,

though they have become meaningless in the political system of modern France since 1870. So some of the pagan
gods were retained as saints in Christian hagiolatry and in
modern America the ancient art of casting horoscopes still
obtains. Such survival is a telling instance of the transformation of instrumental into terminal values.

7. Influence on the arts

Any art which seems to enhance the prestige of the
dominant pattern of culture within a society will be approved by the society in question. Thus painters like
Norman Rockwell, who present the American public with
winsome representations of what they believe to be typi-
cally American life, will meet with wider approval than
painters like Georgia O'Keefe, many of whose pictures are
also representative but non-social in any obvious sense.
Folk-art will emerge, as it has in the United States, to a
level on which critics of a previous generation would never
have placed it, for the nationalistic spirit in the arts in this
country has increased as it had in Scandinavia, Russia, and
the Balkans during the nineteenth century. American folk-
art, in the fields of painting and visual decoration, is to be
sure entirely derivative from early nineteenth century
German and English patterns and motifs. But even when
a Pennsylvanian chest has an inscription in German, it is
still cherished as an authentic product of American culture.
So Maryland furniture, Bostonian silver, and eighteenth
century architecture, both northern and southern, repeat
familiar European originals. But they are approved, in
utter oblivion of their historical origin, as American.

In a stratified society like our own, each stratum will
have its own standards of approbation. There will be
Catholic art, revolutionary art, academic art, the art of
the *illuminati*, the art of the masses, and so on. Each

stratum will give hearty approval to its own art and de-
nunciation of that of other strata. Few things are more
ironical than the essays written by museum directors on
the popular arts of their cities, or by the citizens of
Bohemia on the art of Philistia. Each makes the usual
mistake of believing in the homogeneity of human nature
and wondering why, when all men are so fundamentally
alike, their tastes are so different. One wonders why it
would not be as simple to argue that since men's tastes
are different, so are men.[3]

[3] In corroboration of what has been said, it is pleasant to record the
following: "One need not assume . . . that human nature is unchanging in its basic social traits in order to proceed upon this assumed similarity to ascribe motives and passions to ancient Greeks
and Romans similar to those which prevail in his (*sic*) own conditioned cultural life. Rather, the fact that individuals are culturally
conditioned in diverse ways, a fact established by descriptive social
sciences in our own day, argues against supposing more than a
similarity of sentient organism—a physiological sameness of need for
food, of sex-drives, and of capacity to suffer and enjoy."—Edward
W. Strong, "Fact and Understanding in History," *Journal of Philosophy*, XLIV, no. 23, Nov. 6, 1947, p. 623.

CHAPTER EIGHT

THE HIERARCHY OF VALUES

1. *Historical note*

THE ARRANGEMENT of things in a hierarchical order is so customary that we often lose sight of its metaphorical nature. To say that one kind of thing is "higher" or "lower" than another seems reasonable and the problems which it presents do not seem obvious. Yet the technique of thinking which it involves is not self-justified nor is the meaning of higher and lower clear. In all probability the concept arose first, as the etymology of the word would seem to indicate, in a hierarchy of power. The classical Greek priesthood was not organized into a hierarchy; each individual priest served his own god in independence of other priests. The likelihood is that the notion came into the western world from Asia Minor or Egypt, for the first extended use of the terms occurs in Pseudo-Dionysius the Areopagite.[1] A hierarchy of power is easily enough understood. As in an army, one has corporals in charge of squads, sergeants in charge of platoons which are made up of squads, captains in charge of companies which are made up of platoons, and so on up to Army Groups. Each higher rank connotes actual, not figurative, power, as well as control over the ranks which are lower. The individual who is at the apex of the

---

[1] The idea was used of course much earlier by Philo Judaeus and in the third century by Plotinus. But Pseudo-Dionysius is probably the source of its popular usage.

pyramid has power over everyone below. We see such an arrangement in the Roman Catholic or in fact in any episcopal church, in the feudal system as it existed in theory, and in Heaven, the Church, and Earth according to Pseudo-Dionysius.

In the logic of Aristotle, all things fell into classes which were included in larger classes until one finally reached the most inclusive class of all. The scheme of the logical hierarchy was worked out in detail at least as early as the third century A. D. in the famous Tree of Porphyry. We are familiar with its application to science in such fields as botany and zoology, where varieties, species, genera, families, orders, are commonplace. This scheme of things had been identified in practice by Porphyry's teacher, Plotinus, with a hierarchy of reality, in which God or the One was at the apex of the pyramid and matter at its base.

Whereas it is obvious that in a hierarchy of power the higher ranks may be called better than the lower, if value is to be measured by power, it is by no means obvious that in a hierarchy of logical classes the same is true. No one would believe without proof that a genus was inherently better than a species. And when it comes to a belief in a hierarchy of reality, based on the notion that some things are more real than others, it is questionable whether anyone who had not been submitted to a course in metaphysics would even imagine that the adjective " real " admitted of degrees. No one would deny that some things are real and some unreal, but few would admit without previous indoctrination that, for instance, a stone was less real than the idea of a stone.

In Plotinus the three hierarchies were fused and identified. Thus at the top was the most real, most general, best, and most beautiful; at the bottom the least real, most concrete, worst, and ugliest. And since God was at

the top and matter at the bottom, the former being perfectly active, the latter utterly inert, the ancient and
primitive meaning of a hierarchy, that of power, was
retained.

2. The hierarchies of power

In modern western society there are three hierarchies
of power which have influence upon the arts. They are
represented in the priesthood, the political system, and
the social hierarchy. The priestly hierarchy running from
catechumens to Pope is familiar enough to everyone to
require no exposition here. The political hierarchy is less
clear-cut, but most people are no doubt familiar with its
exemplification in the precinct bosses, the district bosses,
the city bosses, state bosses and national bosses. In the
feudal system the arrangement was clearer: thus in the
English nobility one can run down from the King through
the royal dukes, the non-royal dukes, the marquises, earls,
viscounts, and barons, none of whom have any adminis-
trative function invested in their rank—except on certain
ceremonial occasions—but who historically did have such
functions. The social hierarchy is still less precise and in
America less overtly recognized. But in every society
there are tacitly admitted ranks, social classes which an
anthropologist could sort out and arrange from lower to
higher, as Professor Lloyd Warner has done so neatly in
his various studies. Just how the upper-upper class is
distinguished from the upper class and that from the
middle and that from the lower-middle and so on to the
lower-lower may vary from community to community,
here depending on ancestry, there on wealth, in some
cases possibly on intelligence or service to the City. But
in all cases the upper ranks have influence upon the lower,

not by overtly giving them orders which must be obeyed, but by more subtle control which is just as effective.

3. *The hierarchy of social prestige*

The hierarchy of social prestige runs down from the most respected people in a community to the gutter-snipes, from those people whose approval is sought by everyone, whose manners, speech, taste, amusements, ways of entertainment, have authority and constitute a standard for almost all others.[2] What is " done," and what not done are determined by this hierarchy. It may not be and often in American society is not identical with the hierarchy of political power. No one wants to imitate the speech of the politically powerful and no one thinks that the aesthetic taste of an arch-bishop is any better than that of a parish priest. In Japan the two hierarchies became sharply separated. The hierarchy of power ran up to the Shogun, the hierarchy of prestige up to the Emperor. One had the court-nobility on the one hand, the feudal lords on the other, and, though it is probable that both had a certain prestige, that of the court was not based on actual political power. The Emperor was in the hands of the Shogun politically. So in the older cities of the United States, those who wield social power, in the vague sense of being the arbiters of the elegancies, are far from wielding political power, except when they use their prestige to influence the decisions of statesmen.

4. *The biological hierarchy*

The biological hierarchy came into existence when the theory of organic evolution caused some people to believe that taxonomy was a picture of how species developed.

[2] " Almost " because when one gets low enough, the upper-upper class meets with contempt and derision.

The basis for this was the logical hierarchy, but some evidence was produced—enough to modify western thinking considerably—to show that the higher classes developed out of the lower, came upon the scene later in world-history, and somehow or other included the lower—as suggested in the so-called Law of Recapitulation. There was already in Aristotle's biology a hint of this, in his theory that animals were sensitive plants and men rational animals. Men were everything that plants and animals were and more. In view of Aristotle's additional theory that the lower orders existed for the sake of the higher, one can see why the higher were thought of as inherently better than the lower.[3] It is very difficult to see how the higher animals are concretely any better than the lower animals. Each animal or plant would seem to demand special valuation in such terms as that of fitness to survive, adaptation to environment, plasticity, and the like. But no doubt the observation that the evolutionary series seemed to terminate in man—which in reality it does not, for the marine mammals would appear to be later than human beings—and since man naturally thinks that he is the goal of life, each step towards man, one imagines, would be thought of as an ascent in value as well as in complexity or plasticity or adaptibility.

5. *The dialectical hierarchy*

The evolutionary process during the nineteenth century was confused with the dialectical hierarchy by Hegel and his school. In Hegel's works the earlier stages of development, whether biological, political, intellectual, aesthetic, were primitive not merely in the sense of being first, but

[3] For a full account of the history of this idea and its ramifications, its philosophic basis, and its effects on thinking in general, see A. O. Lovejoy's *The Great Chain of Being.*

in the sense of being rudimentary, inchoate elements of what was to come. The later stages were " implied " in the earlier as logical consequences are implied in their antecedents, and thus could be looked on as the very inherent purpose of the earlier. Thus all history had a goal and that goal was made real step by step, going from worse to better, from least true to most true, from least real to most real. So in the Marxist scheme, there is a necessary historical passage from the lower forms of socio-economic organization to the higher, and the adjectives *lower* and *higher* connote *worse* and *better*. Neither Hegelian nor Marxist would maintain that the earlier stages of history could have been improved at the date of their appearance on this planet; the evil consists in attempting to return to them, or to keep them alive at a later date, for each stage of development is fitting only for the date at which it first occurs.

6. *The causal hierarchy*

Whereas the dialectical hierarchy is a fusion of logic and history, the causal hierarchy is pure history. It takes, however, various forms. Thus it may run from the universal cause, or first cause—in one of the many senses of " first "—to the most specific causes. Or it may run from matter, to living matter, to human life, somewhat by analogy to Comte's classification of the sciences from the most inclusive to the most specific, the latter of which in spite of their specificity absorbing the method and including the subject-matter of the earlier. The causal hierarchy may thus run from beginning to end or from end to beginning. For when one identifies the first cause with God, one is clearly not going to make His remote influences better in any sense than He is. But if one identifies it with matter, the reverse will be true.

7. *The sensory hierarchy*

The last hierarchy which should be indicated as of interest to a theory of aesthetic criticism is the hierarchy of the senses. We find Mr. Santayana in an early book, *The Sense of Beauty*, maintaining that the human senses may be divided into the lower, touch, taste, and smell, and the higher, sound and sight. Why there should be this discrimination, he does not tell us. Is it because the lower senses seem more animal than the higher ? But after all dogs have more acute hearing than men and hawks more acute vision. Do they seem more bodily ? But though touch and taste demand bodily contact with their stimulus, smell does not; and even the higher eyes and ears require some material contact with their objects. Mr. Santayana, as is his practice, gives us no justification of his prejudices.

8. *The values attached to the levels*

The whole matter of hierarchies becomes of interest to criticism only because each level is believed to be marked off from others by its possession of a degree of value which none other possesses. The higher senses are supposed to be inherently better than the lower and consequently such assertions as that the pleasures of vision are nobler than those of taste, or that painting is inherently higher than cooking, appear to make sense. In a social hierarchy the distinction becomes clearer, because one sees the practical effect of the greater prestige of the higher levels in human conduct. In the days when social rank was correlative with political power, rank in itself was a measure of nobility, privileges as well as rights were granted to each rank as such. So today, even in countries which pride themselves on their contempt for this sort of thing, the higher ranking officers of the Army or Navy do not merely

have more power, but also more privileges, privileges
which are due to a certain level, even when the individuals
seated on that level are not the most admirable specimens
of the human race.[4] One is told that such sneers are quite
out of place, as indeed they are if the basic theory is true;
that one is not granting a good billet, a good car, a boot-
black and table servant, and so on to John Doe, the person,
but to General John Doe, the officer. Even in the biological hierarchy, it is presumed that the characters of the
higher animals are inherently better than those of the
lower. It is doubtless true that one of the reasons for this
is that men would prefer to be men than fishes or quad-
rupeds. But aside from this question of taste, and it has
been a disputed taste at best,[5] the rational animality of
the human race is flatly asserted to be better than the
sensitive animality of the beast, which in turn is asserted
to be better than the reproductive and nutritive functions
of the vegetables. Though we shall not indulge in the
futile discussion of whether animals or men are better off,
or whether it would not be better to be a tree than a man,
there has existed enough infra-primitivism in the literary
history of Western Europe to demonstrate that the hierarchical valuation of the various kingdoms of creation is
no more than an assumption.

What is of more importance for our purposes is the
actual fact that when such a hierarchy is accepted, then
anything which is intimately associated with a level will
take on the value of that level, as the wives of kings in
certain countries become queens upon their marriage, even
though they may have been commoners before.

For that reason the arts which enhance, or express, the

---

[4] Cf. the popular slogan in the U. S. Navy, *RHIP*—" Rank hath its
privileges."

[5] See the author's *The Happy Beast, passim.*

values of the various levels will acquire the values of those levels. In a hierarchy of power, courtly arts will be considered higher than popular arts; in a hierarchy of social evolution, the arts of the most evolved society will become higher than those of the lower societies; and similarly the most highly evolved art will be considered better than one less developed. In a causal hierarchy, the most general cause, love or economic desires, for instance, will become higher than less general causes and love stories, or stories depicting the economic struggle, will be thought of as more serious, more worthwhile, more enlightening, more profound—no matter how boring they may be—than those which treat of interests which are believed to be less basic. None of the assertions involved in critical statements of this type are ever proved—nor do I say that they ever could be—but it appears that the universal is better than the particular and consequently an art expressive of universal appetites, universal misfortunes, universal aspirations, is supposed to be better than one that is not. It is usually admitted that in works of art the universal is expressed through the particular, for try as one will, one cannot write a novel without a semblance of human beings running through it. One cannot paint the universal apple except in particular guise. But the emotional effect of imagining that the particularity of one's subject-matter has turned into a universal is apparently very strong.

9. *Three examples*

a) *Tragedy versus comedy*   I know of no literary hierarchy giving every form of writing its rank, but is seems to be common belief that certain forms can be compared on the basis of inherent value. The most familiar example of this is the relative value given to tragedy and comedy. In Aristotle it was inevitable that tragedy be the nobler

form of writing, since he believed that it dealt with nobler
people and with their fate, whereas comedy dealt with
the lower orders. And indeed, though we have lost the
major portion of Greek dramatic literature, it would look
as if his observation applied accurately to what is left.
The plays of Aristophanes not only make their characters
appear ridiculous, but their characters are themselves
ridiculous people, stewards, sausage makers, slaves, para-
sites, paid teachers (Sophists), who were supposed to be,
as one can see from Aristotle's comments, of a lower rank
than the princes, heroes, legendary chieftains and demigods of the tragedies. The tradition that great men,
princes and nobles, were inherently finer than small people,
the *petite bourgeoisie*, as they would probably be—in-
accurately—called now, is indicated in Aristotle's famous
remark that a man who engages in retail trade is incapable
of leading a life of virtue. If there are subject-matters
which can be arranged in a hierarchy of value, it goes
without saying that the works of art which embody or
express or even represent the various subject-matters
have the same values or might at least be imagined to.
(It might of course be theoretically possible that of two
plays, one comic and one tragic, for instance, Addison's
Cato and Congreve's *The Way of the World*, the comedy
would be so much better a specimen of comedy than the
tragedy is of tragedy that critics would be a bit uneasy
about ranking *Cato* above *The Way of the World*.) Logically, the situation would reduce to this: the worst
tragedy is better than the best comedy. The difficulty
in discussing such a question is that one does not know
whether tragedies are those plays which are called
tragedies or whether there is a tragic essence which exists
apart from all plays and whose nature may be intuited by
the critic. If the latter alternative is correct, then of course

there is no denying that the plays which are really tragic are by that very fact inherently better than those which are really comic, granted the hierarchy.

There may indeed be some people who have the gift for intuiting these aesthetic essences, who can spot in the Platonic heaven the tragic, the comic, the pathetic, the farcical, the melodramatic, the mock-heroic, and can then discover their presence or their absence in a given work of art. But judging from their disputes with one another, the gift is very rare and the disputes incapable of settlement, for those who possess the former seem never able to transmit their visions to others.

b) *The Wagnerian theory of opera* The prose writings of Wagner contain an essay on the opera in which that form of composition is given the highest place among the various arts on the grounds that it is all inclusive. For clearly an opera contains, or may contain, acting, poetry, music, painting—in the stage settings, dancing, and architecture. Though no work of art is purely anything, for dancing is also painting when seen and is usually accompanied by some kind of music, and even music, sometimes thought of as the purest of the arts, contains elements of dramatic conflict—see especially the later quartettes of Beethoven, yet some forms of art are, it must be granted, less inclusive than the Wagnerian operas. But the very necessity to include so much is a severe limitation on the composer. Why did Brahms never complete an opera ?

The hierarchy of inclusiveness has never been logically applied and such an application would probably dissuade one from its use. One would be forced to conclude that the Saint Matthew Passion should be ranked lower than *Lohengrin* because it is less of a spectacle. Beethoven's

Opus 131 would be lower than Verdi's *Il Trovatore*. More-over, there are few people who are so appreciative and so catholic in their tastes that they can take in all that is before them in a Wagnerian opera. It is doubtful whether the average person who enjoys hearing their music can catch enough of their words to know whether they are great poetry or not and, certainly if one may judge from the way in which they are usually staged, not even the producers know much about what painters would consider to be satisfactory spectacles, Bayreuth to the contrary. Far be it from one who prefers Mozart to Wagner and the *Odyssey* to the *Nibelungenlied* to proffer his opinion as authoritative in this matter. But if in-clusiveness is the test, then a three ring circus would be even greater than the *Goetterdaemmerung*. For there one has added to everything in the opera, the clowns, the acro-bats, the jugglers, to say nothing of the trained animals which put even Lohengrin's swan to shame and are rivaled only by the elephants in *Aida*.

c) *Realism versus idealism* The battle here is joined on the issue of truth to " life." " Life " is one of those words which had better be banished from the aesthetic lexicon, for everything which a man does is part of it and it serves to distinguish nothing whatsoever from anything else, except death. When a realist says that the idealist is not true to life, the idealist might very well retort that life contains ideals. But " life " has not been banished and everyone still talks as if he knew what was life and what was non-life. I suppose that the idealistic program goes back to a kind of Neo-Platonism, in which the artist is held to express not that which exists in time and space but those universal ideas which transcend the dimensions of existence. Poetry was for this reason ranked above

history by Aristotle, for the latter clearly had to depict
things whose dates were important; it discussed the war
between Athens and Sparta, the career of Alcibiades, the
decline of the Persian Empire. Poetry would presumably
brush aside the particularity of such events and discuss
war, not any particular war, the Dissolute Politician, and
the Fall of Empires. How one could do the latter without
presenting its subject-matter in concrete—even if imagin-
ary—form is hard, if possible, to conceive. Orestes, Oedipus, Antigone, are presented as actual people and their
dramatic problems are presented as those of persons. The
Oedipus story is not a treatise on filial relations, in spite
of Freud, but is used as such by commentators. Moreover,
in spite of what such commentators say, when we see the
universal in the Oedipus story, we know perfectly well that
we are abstracting from it some of the incidents which the
Greeks believed to be historically true: the oracle, the
exposure of Oedipus, the riddle, the actual, not symbolical,
incest, the blinding of Oedipus. Such a purgation makes
it possible for us to interpret *Hamlet* as another instance
of the same theme. But no oracle told Hamlet that he
was to kill his father—in fact, he has a certain hesitation
in killing his uncle, to marry his mother, to live from
babyhood to manhood in foreign parts, to be blinded and
wander for years over the face of the earth, nor do any
of these things happen. Even if Hamlet is in love with
his mother, which is by no means certain, that would be
the only similarity between the two stories. And consequently we could conclude that since every man is in
love with his mother, the two plays deal with universal
themes. But in that case *Oedipus* and *Hamlet* as well
reduce to the following sentences: *A Greek prince was in
love with his mother*, and *A Danish prince was in love*

with his mother. If those sentences are tragedies, then the two plays are identical. And if such universal truths are more important than the complete stories given in both plays, so very different from each other, so exquisitely related to the cultures in which they arose, so thoroughly motivated by the religious, the moral, the psychological sense of their times, then what is the point in reading all the pages which dwell precisely on what must be irrelevant ?

On the other hand, the realist of the sort who maintains that particularity, historical verisimilitude, accuracy to fact, are all important would have to maintain also that there is no explaining and making plausible anything that goes on in his plays. For as soon as one explains and renders occurrences intelligible, one has recourse either to science or to what takes its place, common-sense observation of the human race, and in so doing he passes beyond the particular to the general. Both Sophocles and Shakespeare used language, common nouns and adjectives, which apparently were understood by their contemporaries. It seems to be a common trait of mankind to say with Landor's—and Sappho's—young girl, *But Oh, whoever felt as I ?* Yet in spite of our conviction that our feelings are peculiar and unique, we are also convinced that we can make others understand them and we set to work to do so by paradoxically putting them into words which by their very nature cannot articulate unique feelings. If one is sure that one has a unique experience, one can only keep silent about it or at best weep, groan, sigh, smile, pant, dance, clap one's hands. And even then, one runs the risk of being misunderstood. For if a smile means pleasure, it still does not mean my particular and unique pleasure at, for instance, hearing the Sailors' Farewell in *Dido and Aeneas.*

6

What we are trying to indicate is the futility of both programs. Science, which deals in generalities, is no nobler nor inherently better than direct experience, which is dumb. Nor is the latter any better than the former. The absolute realist might paint a picture, but he could never write a word. The absolute idealist might write mathematics, but certainly not what we usually think of as poems. But in any event, it will be the spectator's interpretation of what we do which counts, and that will be based as we have already pointed out above, on his individual preconceptions.

CHAPTER NINE

FACTORS INFLUENCING THE HIERARCHY
OF VALUES

WE HAVE GIVEN examples of various hierarchies
which may find expression in the arts, belief in
which may have determined the actual value which critics
have given to some forms of art. It is now our unpleasant
duty to indicate some of the factors which influence critics
in making their hierarchies, factors which are not resident
in the objective world but are to be found in the minds of
the theorists. Following our practice, we shall discuss
these under two headings, those which may influence
liking and those which may influence approbation, recognizing that the two attitudes in reality are intertwined.

1. *Liking*

a) *The actual intensity of the liking.* It would probably not be disputed that if a person likes something better
than something else, the two things may for purposes of
discussion be arranged along a scale of preference or value.
Thus if I prefer *Hamlet* to *Othello* and *Othello* to *A
Winter's Tale* and *A Winter's Tale* to *Measure for
Measure*, assuming that one can like and dislike anything
as complicated as a whole play, then I have established
a hierarchy of values without reflection and without
theoretical considerations. If now I find that I like to
read Shakespeare better than I like to read Dryden, and
Dryden better than Otway, and Otway better than

151

Stephen Phillips, assuming again that one can prefer a whole author as a lump to another author—an assumption which is probably untrue to fact, then again I have established a hierarchy, not of works of art but of artists. If finally I find that I prefer to read poetic tragedies, regardless of who wrote them, to prose comedies, regardless of who wrote them, and prose comedies to problem plays and problem plays to historical dramas, my preference has built up a third hierarchy, of kinds of works of art. These hierarchies are by hypothesis based upon the intensity of my liking and I am assuming that I really know what I like and how much I like it.

But lest it be believed that we stand by so naive a psychology, let it be repeated that it seems scarcely possible for anyone to like and dislike anything as big as a whole play, to say nothing of an author or a *genre*. One can like and dislike individual sentences or figures of speech or possibly total paragraphs which are grasped as perceptual units. But to apprehend a whole play as a unit of this sort would demand a kind of synoptic perception which could be brought about only by constantly re-reading the play in question, remembering it in all its detail, and in all likelihood eliminating certain portions as unessential. It makes sense to say that a man prefers dry wines to sweet or even meat to fish or the society of one person to another, though even here it is doubtful whether any human being is entirely detestable, or entirely lovable. What actually happens is that one's first association with a long book or a human being is, let us say, unpleasant; we are then discouraged from continuing our association and thus never discover whether a repetition of the experiment might be more pleasurable. However great one's liking—I am not speaking of approbation —of *Hamlet* may be, there are certainly incidents in the play which seem absurd or grotesque or boring to an unprejudiced mind. If this were not so, the play would not be produced with so many cuts. But we are deliberately eliminating such considerations in order to simplify our argument.

Now though it is possible for a man with a certain amount of insight into his own tastes to generalize and declare what he likes and what he dislikes, he himself seldom knows why his desires run along the course they take. Horses may prefer hay to fish and timothy to nettles, but they have no idea of why this is so. One should have to be a psychologist to understand the roots of our preferences and even the psychologist is still at the beginning of his science. If, however, the psychological laws were clear and well founded and if they were capable of generalization, so as to apply to all men in a given society, then one could with confidence speak of a hierarchy of likings applicable to a certain portion of the human race.

b) *The ground for generalization* No generalizations can be made about any class of objects unless the members of the class are homogeneous. This linguistic truism is not so silly as it seems. For we lump things together because of one set of common properties which will give them their name and then conclude that they must have other common properties. It is to be sure obvious that if human beings did not have some traits in common they would not have been called by the same name, *human beings*. But the question is whether their humanity is such that from its traits can be deduced general principles on the basis of which we can erect a hierarchy of preferences which will be found to be pervasive of the class. If such homogeneity existed, common sense observations about the differences in taste would not have been formulated.[1] If at a given time some men preferred Poussin to Rubens and others with equal intensity preferred Rubens to Poussin, it is certain that the difference in taste did not arise from the human traits which the two groups had in common.

There would seem to be one preference which all human beings exhibit, that is, a liking for pornography. There are individuals who dislike obscenity intensely, but on the whole there are fewer dissenters in this field than in others. And yet even here what is considered obscene in one group or at one time is not so considered elsewhere and at other times. How much of this dislike is really disapprobation, one does not know, though one may have one's own ideas on the subject. But certainly no other human interest seems so wide-spread as the pornographic, appearing in ancient and modern, in primitive and advanced, in oriental and in occidental art. Every level of society has its own form of preferred obscenity and, if one may judge from one's own experience, every individual has his. On the basis of universal liking, one might easily infer that the highest form of art is the obscene.[2]

Generalizations about human likes and dislikes could also be based upon the social patterns in which human beings live. Since much of our liking is the product of social approbation, and since the latter is a function of the social structure, or of the structure of the class with

---

[1] See the anthology of literary masterpieces edited by Huntington Cairns, *The Limits of Art*, in which even serious and highly respected crtiics apply the same superlatives to several examples of prose and poetry. They obviously cannot all be right.

[2] Every civilized society has also had its mystical literature which is more homogeneous in its mode of expression than its pornographic. But of course it is not so wide-spread within the society.

which we identify ourselves for one reason or another, it would follow that in a highly organized and simple society liking would be fairly homogeneous. There would, however, always be rebellious individuals even there, but we can overlook them for the moment. But contemporary American society is far from homogeneous. In 1940 there was an urban population of 74 millions and a rural population of 57 millions. Over ten percent. of the people were foreign born. Over eleven percent. were non-Caucasians. As for education one third of the adults had been only to grade schools, fifteen percent. had been to high school, and only a little over five percent. had been to college. And everyone knows how dissimilar the curricula of each of these categories of school are in the various communities. Though over $48 million were earned in manufacturing, $26 million were earned in government jobs, $13 million in agriculture, and so on. Religiously the country in 1945 had over 72 million churchgoers, of whom 24 million were Roman Catholics and the others Protestants, Jews, Greek Orthodox, and so forth. However inaccurate and vague these statistics are, and they are highly questionable in certain respects—such as meaning of the terms, nevertheless they indicate how diverse the population is in those very respects which might be held to determine tastes. One can scarcely expect an adult of the age of 25 who has never gone beyond the eighth grade to like what a university graduate likes, nor an agricultural worker to like what a bank clerk or a federal employee likes. One can scarcely expect a Roman Catholic to read with pleasure Anatole France's *Histoire Contemporaine*, nor an orthodox Jew to prefer to spend his leisure reading the poems of Paul Claudel. It may be maintained that these differences are superficial and that underneath the working man, the college professor, the

Catholic, the farmer, lies the human being. That is better rhetoric than science. No one denies that each of these people has to live, eat, love, and think, but the emotional tone of these interests will vary from person to person, not merely because of his inherent psychological and physiological makeup, but because of the social groups with which he is identified. For in the long run a man is not a Catholic merely by chance, nor even merely by inheritance; he is not a Catholic simply because he belongs to a certain income-group nor because his glandular equipment is what it is. A matter of belief is involved. This belief will determine not only his remaining a Catholic, but also determine what he feels about sexual activity, gluttony, mendacity, charity, sloth, envy, and pretty nearly everything else. And if one ask which comes first, the man or the working man, the man or the Catholic, the man or the educated man, the question remains unanswered because it is meaningless. One cannot be born just a man. One is born into a certain family which already has its social linkages, to bodies religious, economic, political, aesthetic, and so on. One's history subsequent to birth is neither entirely determined by one's family nor entirely free from one's family; it is often a reciprocal set of influences.

c) *The social control of our biological drives.* It is for that reason that we cannot assert that the biological drives have a pre-eminent position in life, for though our innate desires or our instincts, if there are any, may be common to all humanity, none of them is allowed to satisfy itself without social supervision and even control. There exists no society which does not determine when and how a man shall eat, procreate his kind, defend his wife and children and himself, hold property, buy and sell, amuse himself. One absorbs one's standards of decency and indecency, one's sense of sin and innocence, from one's companions. The very language which we use is determined by the groups in which we move, one set of words being decent at home, another at work, one set in the company of women, another in the company of men, a third in the company of children. One did certain things in the Army and Navy which one would never think of doing in civil life, things which seemed not only not bad but actually desirable. Who in civil life in America moves about in blind obedience to his superiors? Who would dream of entering a person's house, requisitioning it, burning the furniture for warmth, stealing cameras and watches, insulting women on the streets, and all the while puffing out his chest and feeling specially manly? Critics of our behaviour during combat and the occupation of Germany—to say nothing of the occupation of England and France—laid the blame on American schooling and at times even on American religion. The answer was simply that the soldier during war is neither at school nor in church.

Thus approbation is so closely associated with liking that it will influence the satisfaction of those biological drives which are necessary for man's continued existence. No society nor social group could be expected to flatly deny their satisfaction, but all control the manner of their satisfaction, establish habits which become compulsive in certain contexts, and thus create the feeling of necessity or horror which seem to the naive mind evidence of their " natural " status.

2. *Approbation*

But since approbation is always expressed in laws and rules and codes and commandments and hence has a kind

of existence which appears to be separate from conduct—
as indeed it is in its literary form—one can study these
principles by themselves as one would study a set of
logical propositions.

a) *An example of a hierarchy of approbation*   I have
chosen for this purpose an example of a hierarchy of values
which is clear and which seemed to at least its author, a
man of great experience and wisdom, reasonable and
perhaps even obvious. The late Professor W. G. Everett
in his book, *Moral Values* (p. 182) gives the following
hierarchy, running from worse to better to best.

The interest	*Locus of the value*
Economic	Wealth
Bodily	Health
Recreation	Play
Association	Sympathy, friendship
Character	Temperance, truthfulness, benevolence
Aesthetic	Beauty
Intellectual	Wisdom
Religious	Feeling of submission to the world-order, sense of harmony and co-operation with it, faith and hope in the triumph of the good, delight in the divine law

Many people educated in the Neo-stoicism of the American universities would accept this hierarchy as indicating
the scale of things which they ought to prefer, whether
they do or not. They would believe, whatever their conduct may show, that wisdom is preferable to beauty,
beauty preferable to a good character, a good character
preferable to athletic skill, athletic skill preferable to
health, in so far as one can have the one without the
other, and all of them preferable to money. Just what
was the basis of Mr. Everett's scale does not appear from
his book, but in it one sees a principle of gradation at

work. It appears to be the inclusiveness of that from which the value arises. Thus the lower values arise in the individual's own life; wealth is one's own, so is health. One then passes on to those which can be enjoyed only in the presence of others; play, sympathy, temperance and truthfulness, benevolence. Finally we have a group whose field runs from the panorama of nature to the universe as a whole. This principle is not without its weaknesses, for one cannot acquire wealth except in society, though one can enjoy it in defiance of society. Similarly one finds beauty usually in the external world, but there are some people who might prefer their dreams. Yet in spite of these qualifications, the hierarchy is one which is intelligible and which, with the exception of the religious level, would be acceptable to at least one stratum of American society.[3]

b) *The rôle of society in determining the hierarchy*
Even within this group it will be observed that though the values sought will be found only in society, they will not be conferred on the individual by society. On the lowest level, the wealth which a man earns is not given him by others; others simply permit him to make it and keep it, and admire him for having made it and kept it. One cannot be healthy without hundreds of others, from the producers of food to the physicians, to work for one; but society does little if anything to make a man healthy, except in so far as he might acquire a contagious disease or otherwise be a menace to the health of others. But once he has become healthy, society will admire him for it and may even reward him, a reward which may consist simply in the admiration which is bestowed on a healthy

[3] A conclusion based on trying it out on successive classes of undergraduates. But there have always been dissenters.

specimen of humanity.[4] The most that society will do for the attainment of values is to contribute the pattern in which the values are to be achieved, a competitive or co-operative pattern, the occasions for achieving them, and the prestige for having achieved them.

For example, in modern America, whatever may be the situation elsewhere, society as a whole will tolerate a variety of religious beliefs and rites, but it has no pretension of determining what those beliefs and rites should be. It might even go to the extent of guaranteeing their existence in the face of opposition, as when it permits members of the Society of Friends to escape conscription in time of war. But it will not decide whether one should be a conscientious objector or not—though in actual practice enough pressure is brought to bear on conscientious objectors by individuals to result in their unhappiness. It will guarantee a certain freedom in aesthetic matters, but will not choose one set of aesthetic practices to the exclusion of others. It has a tendency to remain open, to rebel against institutionalism, though it must be admitted that in the United States the counter-pull is growing steadily and the state is tending to take the place of an " open society."[5]

On every level of Mr. Everett's hierarchy governments, either the federal or the state or the municipal, interfere with the satisfaction of one's desires, acting as if the state were a social group, or in fact the dominant social group, whereas it is nothing of the sort, but simply a selected number of individual men and women who change their rôle as servants of society into the rôle of governors of

---

[4] Cf. the admiration bestowed on women who were unhealthy—delicate—in the early nineteenth century America.

[5] It would be interesting to learn how this movement is related to the steady growth of organized religion.

society. Thus we maintain that we have a free economic order, but we cannot earn money as we will. Some occupations are outlawed, such as prostitution, gambling, fortune-telling, combinations in restraint of trade; others are protected by tariffs and subsidies, such as most manufactures, agriculture, shipping, aviation; the size of fortunes is regulated by income taxes and inheritance taxes. One's bodily interests again are supposed to be freely satisfied, but most communities have compulsory vaccination and innoculation against epidemics; compulsory sanitary inspection of houses and public buildings; there is inspection of meat which is put on sale; drugs and foods have to be properly labeled. In the City of Baltimore one's play is supervised by the municipal government and if one wished to play tennis in a public park with a negro, one would be violating a law; one cannot walk on the grass of certain public parks; one cannot swim in certain ponds; one cannot shoot craps anywhere, in public or private. As for friendship and the values of social intercourse, there are ten or twelve states in which negroes and whites cannot associate in public, eat in the same restaurants, go to the same theatres together, attend the same lectures, frequent the same schools. Though there is as yet little governmental control of the values of character, the value of benevolence, to take but one example, has been turned over to public organizations, such as the Community Chests which in the long run determine not only where benevolence shall be given but also in what degree, and where private charity once was expected to take care of the aged and the indigent, that is now the function of the state. One may be punished for intemperance, not merely by the physiological sequelae of drunkeness, but by imprisonment. In some states the government makes the decision of who is to drink alcoholic beverages and who not. As for sexual indulgence, no comment is needed. Though the government of the United States has not as yet taken sides in the disputes between artistic *côteries,* yet it spends its money on what might fairly be called conservative art, rather than on that of the advanced guard, and indeed this is true that official art is beginning to be recognized as a distinctive style in America as it has been for many years in France. The state moreover always interferes when its officials decide that a given book or picture or piece of sculpture or play is obscene or indecent, and can prevent its citizens from reading Rabelais or James Joyce for that matter, and in one case on record, Ovid. This has not yet reached the proportions which it reached in Nazi Germany, but there has always been a group of Americans who have felt that taste should be controlled by law, rather than by custom. Our intellectual pursuits in the privately endowed universities are still almost entirely free, but, thanks probably to certain religious bodies more than anything else, the teaching of history and economics and sometimes biology, if not of physics and mathematics, is beginning to feel the whip of the Censor. In times of national collective hysteria, such as the present, only members of certain political parties are permitted to teach in certain state universities, communists being outlawed, as democrats would be outlawed in Russia. And in many a privately endowed university the requirements for teachers include not only scholarship and teaching ability, but also religious, racial, " social," and political affiliations. The United States finally enjoys a multiplicity of religious sects which, one imagines, is unknown elsewhere. But even here the state interferes to the extent of forbidding the Mormons to practice polygamy, faith healers to allow themselves to be bitten by snakes, and, in the state of

Maryland, anyone to work on Sunday.[6] Thus the state erects into statute what is the desire of some of its subjects.

c) *The recalcitrant individuals*   But, it must not be denied, there are always to be found some recalcitrant individuals who follow the technique of rebellion rather than that of resignation. Within such a small society as that of the family, or the larger society of the school, or even within so powerful a group as that of businessmen or manufacturers, some individuals arise who find it as impossible, or as inexpedient, to agree to the demands of the group as the conscientious objector finds it impossible to go to war. Such people have been known to violate the law rather than conform. Whether their action springs from some queer psychological twist which puts a greater value upon self-assertion than upon self-abnegation, whether it arises from conviction based upon reason, whether it arises from loyalty to a group within the larger group which is at odds with the larger group, the recalcitrant are those to whom society owes whatever progress it has made. In the field of science it is they who see problems which are at most trivial exceptions to the rule in the eyes of the great majority and for some reason or other feel it imperative, regardless of ridicule or other forms of punishment, to work towards the solution of such problems. At times like the present, one finds some of them among the programmatic conservatives who in the name of an older tradition refuse to accept what has already become the modern tradition. Only a few years ago writers like Charles Maurras and Léon Daudet in France and Messrs. Babbitt and More in the United States were preaching an ethical and social philosophy which had as its aesthetic implications a new idea and a radical de-

---

[6] In fact, Maryland is distinguished by forbidding civil weddings.

parture from what they believed to be the dominant
modes of thought in their countries and which they believed also to be sanctified by tradition. They were in
their time, like Mr. T. S. Eliot in ours, admitted conservatives, but they were also trying to conserve something
which they confessed had been abandoned some three
hundred years previously. If the correct behaviour for a
man is obedience to tradition, then clearly the duty of the
modern man is to follow the tradition of what may loosely
be called the Renaissance. For even in such a country
as France, which is religiously Catholic, it had been impossible since 1600 to be teleological in science or uni-
versalistic in culture. One might believe in one God, a
fusion of the metaphysical First Cause and the Judeo-
Christian Jehovah, but one could not believe that Shakespeare, Ariosto, and Corneille wrote works which would
have been intelligible to either Philo Judaeus or Saint
Thomas Aquinas, to say nothing of Confucius. The occur-
rence of dissent from the dominant cultural pattern is no
less real because it is voiced in the language of conformity.
But the obvious truth is that conformity is not the goal
of such writers, for there is as much evidence of a non-
classical tradition in ancient times as there is of a classical.
Maurras, and now Mr. Eliot, selected from the traditions
of the past twenty five hundred years those beliefs which
they now hold, and conceal their radicalism by refusing to
recognize the multiplicity of men's belief in the past. If
what they really wish is order, then their duty is to
strengthen the order which exists. But on the contrary,
they create disorder exactly as all revolutionaries do and
must do, by destroying faith in that order. And since
their literary gifts and their intelligence are greater than
those of their adversaries, they are more powerful as
influences.

d) *Destruction of the hierarchy through loyalty* But the most ironical feature of any hierarchy of values is that belief in it and loyalty to its demands destroy it. For since men ought to seek the better rather than the worse, they who take their hierarchies seriously will allow the lower appetites to atrophy, the lower forms of art to perish, and even the lower social classes to die for the sake of the higher. But if one pursues health at the expense of wealth, or play at the expense of health, or religion at the expense of science, one will find as a result that even on paper there will be no economic life, no bodily life, no knowledge. The hierarchy of values will have disappeared by the selective process of choice. And since in a hierarchy the lower levels are often the base on which the higher are built, the higher will disappear with the lower. This gloomy event will never take place, except with the disappearance of mankind, for obviously if one satisfies none of one's economic interests, one will not even be healthy, and if one is not in possession of some degree of health, one will neither play nor associate with one's fellows nor paint pictures nor solve scientific problems nor even worship God. If one have a theory that the satisfaction of the higher interests must kill that of the lower, and that the price is none too high (as is preached in such cases as patriotism or religious asceticism) then of course the event is cheerfully accepted and the death of the soul is no tragedy. But few men have been willing to follow logic to that point. The men of the upper social classes will not swell their ranks so that all may be their fellow-nobles, for clearly where all are on top, no one is below. It thus becomes the duty of the lower classes to accept their position in spite of knowing that it is lower. They must learn the beauty of subservience to their betters, since only that subservience will guarantee the existence of their betters. When they retort that they wish to be among the best, they become guilty of a perverse rebellion against a law of ethics which condemns them to be bad in order that others may be good. But though the delights of keeping one's place have been preached to some extent, the cynicism of urging some men to seek the worse so that others may enjoy the better is so great that most believers in a hierarchical society prefer to be inconsistent rather than inhumane.[7]

e) *The resultant problem*   The resultant problem is thus one of changing the basic metaphor by which values are compared. Instead of a hierarchical pyramid, it might be better to adopt a flat system in which the inter-relations of desires and their satisfactions would be plotted. The original metaphor of the hierarchy, derived from a system of power, simply does not hold of values, since not even the religious values control those beneath them. One can orient one's life towards anything: the satisfaction of sexual appetites, worshipping the Earthly Aphrodite, making and looking at nothing but erotica, making one's living by prostitution and pimping, and taking the Karma Sutra as one's Bible. But few real people are so pure in motivation. For even the entirely erotic life would demand the satisfaction of desires non-erotic; even the lover must eat. And if Society, the society of societies, were to guarantee the satisfaction of our purposes, its task would be that of preventing the destruction of any set of values by exclusive loyalty to any other. But that is a task which could never be really accomplished, since some values are by their very nature destructive of others.

f) *Application to aesthetics*   When a hierarchy is es-

---

[7] But see Mr. Richard M. Weaver's *Ideas Have Consequences*, ch. II and Mr. Eliot's *Towards a New Definition of Culture, passim.*

tablished, the arts of achieving the interests on each level will be ranked according to the level of the interests which they satisfy. In the hierarchy of Everett the arts of making money, even by painting pictures or writing sonnets, will be ranked below those of increasing health, friendship, and so on. This would seem to be a fairly reasonable ordering of our arts, since the people who are interested in such problems are those educated in the tradition of the intellectual and religious values. But because of the multivalence of works of art it is quite possible for a picture or a play which has been made in order to increase the income of the artist to become nevertheless a source of the purest delight to someone who is not the the artist. There is reason to believe that Shakespeare wrote for his living and that his plays were devised to fit the actors whom he had at his disposal: the number of women, villains, juvenile leads, comics being limited by the actors trained to play such rôles. But there is no reason why we in 1949 should devote all our attention to his skill in adapting his plots to his players. It may be true that the female parts are brief on the whole because boys acted them, but women have been acting them since 1660, though the practice of using boys did not die until much later.[8] Similarly, Daumier's drawings for *Charivari* were made to earn his living. That did not prevent their having other qualities of more interest to us than perhaps to him. Moreover, if either of these men had produced something which had been a complete economic failure, we should never have heard of it and its " beauty," in the sense of its unqualified sensory pleasantness, would never have been known.

[8] H. Spencer, *The Art and Life of William Shakespeare*, N. Y., 1940, p. 105, quotes a tribute to the boy actor, Edward Kynaston, written by John Downes as late as 1707.

Such phenomena are perhaps infrequent, if not impossible. We know only too well what has happened to the cinema in the United States, because of placing the economic goal above all else. People who enjoy a certain dose of psychology and even philosophy in their dramas, some comment on life which is not too superficial, are dissatisfied with the usual Hollywood film and when they attribute its character to Holywood's desire to make money above all, they may be right. But what they see in the film is usually not its economic value, which they despise, but its superficiality and triviality, and these are caused not by Hollywood's desire to make money but by Hollywood's estimate of what most people want. If they are in error, the error is psychological. After all, the most popular symphonies at the present time would appear to be Beethoven's *Fifth*, Brahms's *First*, and César Franck's *D-minor*, and there still exist musicians who believe these to be " good " music. There is therefore no reason to believe that a work of art enjoyed by a great many people is either better or worse than one enjoyed by few. But there is a certain irony in hearing the claim that great art is universal accompanied by the belief that only the élite appreciate it.

CHAPTER TEN

STANDARDS

1. *What standards measure*

IN POPULAR speech there would appear to be two sorts of standards, those by which we measure facts and those by which we measure values. We say, in speaking of facts, that if certain conditions prevail, then certain effects ought to be observed. If one swallows an aspirine tablet, then one's temperature ought to go down; if the United States rearms, then it will not be attacked; if one is bitten by an anopheles mosquito, one will get malaria. In such cases, we have made certain generalizations about classes of things: the behaviour of the human organism, of nations, of chemicals. We believe our statements to be true of the class as a whole and are willing to admit that no member of the class will always behave as it ought to. Thus some people are more sensitive to aspirine than others; a potential enemy might find a weapon which it believed to be better than anything which the United States might have and would therefore take a chance and attack; if one is bitten by an anopheles mosquito in Sweden, one will not get malaria. Each of these observations introduces qualifying conditions, but do no more than prove that the original formulations were imprecise. But the same thing is true in regard to even scientific laws. The Law of Gravity is given in the text-books as, Weight equals Mass times Acceleration. But since the earth is an oblate sphere and its surface is mountainous, corrections have to be made for

169

latitude and altitude, and when they are made a much
more precise formula is obtained. The corrections, however, are made with a view to obtaining a verification or
corroboration of the law, which stands as a sort of purified
description of what " ought " to be. The words, "on the
whole," " other things being equal," " on the average,"
which appear so often in scientific generalizations, indicate
clearly what is expected of a scientific standard as well as
what it measures. It is expected to be true of what we call
an ideal situation, which is one in which the disturbing elements are absent, and it measures deviations of a particular case from the ideal, or generalized, situation. If the
earth were a perfect sphere with a smooth surface, then
corrections would not have to be made for altitude and
latitude; but it actually is not one. Again, though anopheles mosquitoes live in Sweden and Norway, the ma-
larial bacillus will not incubate in cold climates, so that
one of the " things-that-have-to-be-equal " is the temperature of the place where one is bitten. Our conclusion then
is that in matters of fact standards apply perfectly only to
classes of things or events, not to particular instances.

But the same holds true also of standards of value. An
individual man can be good or bad only in respect to the
standards of human behaviour. Moral laws are written for
all men and are supposed to gain in dignity the more
general they are. We measure our badness by our deviation from this standard and the conception of extenuating
circumstances, though kindly in its effects, is disturbing
to the purity of our ethical systems. We are told that we
want a universal ethics, not a particularistic one. When
we meet with a moral problem, we try to solve it in uni-
versalistic terms, in what Humanity should or should
not do, and what the individual ought to do is to approach
the human goal as closely as possible. This has been the

backbone of such a system as that of Kant, in which the possibility of generalizing conduct is the possibility of establishing an ethics fit, he believed, for human beings. It thus becomes false to say that it is right for Germans to do what is wrong for Frenchmen or that what it is right for John Doe to do is wrong for Richard Roe. But if that is so, then ethical standards are also applicable to classes and not to individuals, except in so far as individuals are members of a given class.

That standards can be no more nor less than this is shown also by the fact that what a single individual person or event does in isolation from everything else—a situation which obviously does not obtain—becomes the characteristic of that class known as a unit-class. The total behaviour of a given man is inexplicable, in the sense that it is *as a whole* unique. Every individual thing is a law unto itself, for even in the case of falling bodies, what happens to any particular falling body as a particular event is outside the law. If a brick is falling off a high building and bounces on a projecting awning or lands on a balcony, it would be absurd to say that the Law of Falling Bodies has been violated. The Law describes the behaviour of all falling bodies, not of any particular falling body. But all falling bodies do not bounce off awnings or land on balconies. It is only to the extent that any falling body resembles, or exemplifies, all falling bodies that it conforms to the Law. Is there any scientist who would pretend to describe all the accidents, all the peculiar circumstances of history? He deals in classes and for that very reason has to subtract from the particulars precisely those characteristics which make them particulars.

In much the same way, moral problems arise when the moral law is violated. If that were not so, then ethics and psychology would be identical. For instance, if it is assumed that men are rational animals and thus might be expected to behave like rational animals, an individual man who lets his reason be swayed by his passions, thus acting irrationally, becomes a moral problem and he is urged—and sometimes forced—to act as all men should act if the theory were true. But as a matter of fact, people —even lawyers—sometimes recognize the difficulty of acting in accordance with the moral law, and in such cases as *crimes passionnels*, the impossibility of doing so. When that is done, the moral critic acts as if the individual under scrutiny were not a man. He makes allowances for the special conditions under which behaviour may deviate from the norm. Aristotle, who was the father of this particular theory, admitted the possibility of a man's acting as if he were not a rational animal; such possibilities would be found in children, in savages, in madmen, that is, in potential men, incomplete men, and monsters. The first group, children, could be expected to profit by training; the others were without the law. It is doubtful whether we should be so lenient in our self-criticism.

2. *Scientific obligation*

Science tends towards the identification of the " ought " with the " is." It brings this tendency to a limit when it achieves mathematical expressions of observed facts. For mathematics is the most generalized of our disciplines, as every Freshman learns, and no one believes that because one quart of water added to one quart of alcohol does not make two quarts of liquid, 2 added to 2 does not give 4. The arithmetical statement is neither about water nor alcohol nor quarts. It is about numbers. Similarly, in a science like chemistry or physics, where such purification of the material, or historical, world has been pretty nearly accomplished, no scientist is disturbed by the behaviour of real, as against ideal, gases, chemically impure substances, or non-laboratory conditions. They are not his subject-matter. Moreover, his ideal conditions give him a norm from which he can successfully measure deviation; he knows how to allow for such things.

Furthermore, were he to observe a growth in deviation, he would set up a new class or make a new and more general law. A good example of the former is seen in the development of the theory of isomeres. It was originally believed that the properties of a substance were dependent entirely upon its chemical constitution. When two specimens of the same composition behaved differently, it was concluded that impurities were present. When this became disproved, the conclusion had to be drawn that some substances of the same composition do not have the same properties. To explain this the theory was developed that the atoms in isomeric substances, though the same, were arranged differently within the molecule. Thus at least two classes of a given substance were set up, called isomeres. An analogous event occurred in the history of chemistry when it was discovered that a given substance might have two atomic weights. Instead of calling each a new substance, sub-classes were set up called isotopes. No chemist, to the best of my knowledge, blamed the isomeres or isotopes for behaving as they did in violation of the law. In the very nature of things he was forced to accept their existence and change his laws. There was left sufficient generality for his purposes.

If, however, deviation should grow to such a point that no two specimens of any substance behaved alike—an impossibility, since if they did, they would not be specimens of anything—then each would have to be given a proper name, not a common name. But there are contexts, outside of science, where this sort of thing occurs. Sodium chloride on the dining table behaves differently from the way it behaves in the laboratory and in fact it is likely to behave in a peculiar way on the palate of each person eating it, some behaving pleasantly, other specimens behaving unpleasantly. John Doe's salt is not Richard Roe's, if the possessive may be taken to indicate salt-on-the-tongue. But this, though it is irrelevant to chemistry, is not irrelevant to cooking and dining, and the question of how much salt should be put in a dish is not one which can be answered for all men. Hence as deviation becomes of interest, as it often does in human affairs, each particular thing or event forms a class of one member and its relation to larger and more inclusive classes becomes finally of little interest. There are probably minimum and maximum amounts of salt which are tolerable to human beings, but within these limits, there is great variation and each person wants the amount which is correct for him, regardless of any " average " or modal amount.

Similarly in the history of human affairs, a war, for instance, is not just a war; it is this or that war. It may be true that wars are all stupid and horrible, but when one is engaged in a particular war, its problems are not those of all wars and its horrors and stupidity are peculiar to it. The horror and stupidity of the Spanish-American War were not the same as those of the Mexican War of 1846, nor can one judge the wisdom—or unwisdom—of one by the other. A conscript in the Civil War might have felt one way and a conscript in World War II might have felt another about his military obligations and both have been right. Both again might have been conscientious objectors and have felt that they should take part in no war whatsoever, regardless of its causes, its purposes, or its chances of success. In that event, he would be judging them as members of the class, *War*, and obviously overlooking what differentiated them. But it is quite conceivable that he should be more interested in their particularity than in what they have in common. To take a different example, one does not fall in love with the class, *Woman*, one falls in love with a particular woman; one does not read the class, *Book*, one reads a particular book; one does not listen to the class, *Sonata*, but to a specific sonata. One may, however improbably, think of his mistress as simply another specimen of womanhood, of *Mme Bovary* as simply a specimen of prose fiction, of Beethoven's *Opus 110* as simply a specimen of the sonata, thus veering towards a scientific attitude. If it is possible to generalize the traits of all women, all novels, all sonatas, then one can also observe to what extent the particular specimen of the class before one differs from them. And consequently one could take the attitude that one's mistress ought to be more like every other woman, that *Mme Bovary* ought to be more like every other novel, and that the *Opus 110* ought to be more like every other sonata. And, always assuming that our generalizations are sound, indeed they ought, if their purpose in existence is to exemplify class-characteristics. The price they will pay for their deviation from type is all that is implied in individuality.

3. *Moral and aesthetic obligation*

Just as a material object ought to obey scientific law if it is to be classified as such and such, so human acts and artefacts ought to conform to certain general class-traits if they are to be given a common name. There is little sense in calling anything theft or murder or mayhem, unless one has defined a group of acts which have something in common; and similarly it would seem reasonable that one should not call musical compositions *sonatas* or poems *sonnets*, unless they all manifest certain common traits.

Historically these class-names have arisen to cover selected properties of human acts and artefacts and then have been retained to cover others. For instance, mayhem was originally an old Anglo-French name meaning an assault whereby a person is deprived of a member which might be useful in self-defence, such as an arm, a leg, or a front tooth. The loss of an ear was not mayhem. But now the term means any bodily mutilation. A sonata was originally any piece of music composed for bowed instruments, as contrasted with a toccata and cantata, for keyed instruments and voice respectively. But originally no one foresaw the ambiguities which would arise as civilization became more complicated and human interests more diverse, and by the inertia of custom the old terms were retained to mean new things. It is probably true that the only similarity between a Brahms piano sonata and one by the elder Scarlatti is is that they are both played on keyed instruments—not bowed instruments. But that is not why they are called sonatas. They are called by that name simply because the word has become ambiguous and no one cares any longer what class-name they are given.

Upon reflection it turns out in the fields of ethics and aesthetics alike that the word *ought* is always instrumental. you wish to reach such and such a goal, then you ought to do this or that. If you wish to write a piece of music for bowed instruments, then you ought to consider the range of such instruments, their harmonic possibilities, their melodic capacities, and so on. Though one can play certain harmonies on a violin by double stopping, there are others which cannot be played, and you ought not to write them into your composition. Similarly, if you wish to achieve a defined end in non-aesthetic conduct, you should follow a defined course. If you wish to be healthy, wealthy, and wise, then go to bed early and early arise. But who is to say whether health, wealth, and wisdom—assuming that they can be all had together—are to be preferred as a general rule to poverty, illness, and ignorance? The normal man in western society will probably be driven to these ends by the approval of his fellows and will thus think that somehow or other they and the proverbial road to them are self-justified and indeed obviously right. But no man is entirely normal in the sense of accepting with unquestioning devotion every end and every means to it, though perhaps there is greater acceptance of at least two of these ends in America than elsewhere, even if the means for reaching them as given in the proverb is less uncritically accepted.

One of the results of social living is the acceptance of certain standards as the characteristics of a " real " member of the group. One is said to be un-American, however much appearances are against it, when one does not subscribe to a set of interpretations of the Constitution of the United States. How an American can be un-American is only a verbal puzzle. It is assumed that everyone possessing American citizenship holds a set of beliefs in spite of the obvious fact that everyone does not. One's duties as a citizen then become the duty primarily of keeping the generic traits pure. Were the formulation of these traits more carefully made, they would include diversity of belief even about freedom of speech; but such formulations are never carefully made and would, one suspects, lose their force if they were. It is to be noted that the same emphasis on generic purity in made by critics of the arts. It is assumed that each work of art falls into a class of similar objects, that each must in the very nature of things exhibit the class-properties—how indeed could it be otherwise?— that at the same time the work of art before one does not. If the object is a sonnet, then clearly it must have the properties of a sonnet; if it does not have these properties, it is obviously not a sonnet. To find the common traits of all poems which have been called sonnets is next to impossible. The number of lines, the stanzaic form, the rhyme-schemes, the subject-matters, have all differed. But that has not prevented critics from talking about good sonnets and bad sonnets, as if they had in mind some genus, unified and unchanging, whose essence they knew. But how could they know the essence of the genus, *sonnet*, except by studying actual sonnets and how could they study actual sonnets except by studying those poems which have been called sonnets?

When the ends achieved by men are unquestioned, then the principle of ritualization will explain why a given way of reaching them takes on terminal value. The obligation demanded by others is paralleled with a feeling of obligation within oneself, a natural enough consequence of habitual behaviour. The best evidence which one has of the purely conventional nature of these rituals is the actual changes which their history manifests. The manner, for instance, in which Ann Radcliffe tells the story of *The Mysteries of Udolpho* is almost entirely different from that in which Virginia Woolf tells the story of *To the Lighthouse,* or, less we be accused of choosing two somewhat peripheral novelists, the manner in which Defoe tells the story of *Moll Flanders* is quite different from the manner in which Mr. William Faulkner tells the story of *The Sound and the Fury.* If Mr. Faulkner's way is the correct way, then Defoe's way is incorrect. But the ways could legitimately be compared only if both were striving to reach the same goal. It will be, oddly enough, assumed by the critic of the type under discussion that both were aim- at the same target since both wrote novels. But the question remains whether Defoe and Mr. Faulkner were more interested in conforming to the general type, *The Novel,* than in writing each his particular novel. The fact that both *Moll Flanders* and *The Sound and the Fury* are called by the same generic name is to be explained, this book maintains, purely on historical grounds.

4. *The standard as a Platonic idea*

Since it cannot be doubted that natural objects fall into classes and thus have generic traits as well as individual traits, and since much of science depends on the scrutiny of these generic traits, it is legitimate to speak about weight, velocity, acceleration, birds, beasts, and fishes, silver, nitrogen, and sulphur, as if we were talking pure mathematics. By refusing to think about those contexts in which even these terms change their meanings, we can think of them as if they had an existence independent of time and place. Every scientist, when he stops to think, knows that the chemical properties of, for instance, silver are those traits which appear when something called silver is subjected to certain tests. If he defines the metal by its atomic weight, 107.88, and speaks of its having a specific gravity of 10.5 at 20 degrees centigrade, he is not denying that it is also used in certain coins, in jewelry, and in knives, forks, and spoons, however contemptuous he might be of the man who would bring that into the conversation. Nor would he expect a silver-tongued orator to have a tongue whose specific gravity was 10.5 at 20 degrees centigrade nor a silver wedding to have an atomic weight of 107.88. He has established definite criteria for defining his subject-matter and he calls that subject-matter " chemistry."

He may, if he has had philosophical training, look upon chemistry as something existing apart from chemicals and chemists and chemical laboratories, and may even think it has an eternal essence, by gazing upon which he can announce what chemistry " really " is and what it is not. What it is historically is the problems which chemists, flesh and blood chemists, have tried to solve; it is neither more nor less than " what chemists do." And when he says that chemists ought to try to exemplify the problems inherent in the essence of chemistry, he will be urging them to solve the problems of the past. Fortunately such men are rare, or we should still be seeking the Philosopher's Stone and the Elixir of Life.

In the field of aesthetics the terminal value of processes seems to be more persistent than in other fields and the right way to paint pictures, write poems, compose music, remains as a standard long after many artists have invented new ways of doing these things. That may be because artistry, like morality, confers a kind of stability on living which, as we have suggested earlier in this book, has a definite instrumental value. Moreover, people increase the respect for stability through the arts, singing the praises of the olden times, the Golden Age, even primitive life. Thus artistry is a stabilizing force in a double manner. By habitual repetition it retains the past and by consciously emphasizing and glorifying the past it serves to enhance its beauty and its sanctity. Inevitably the works of art, that is, the kinds of works of art attained by these practices become also stabilized and we have both the deliberate imitation of ancient works of art and traditionalistic works of art, the makers of which assume without question that the way of their masters is the right way. The meaning of " right " reduces to " unquestioned " and any end or process which is unquestioned becomes standardized and automatically is metamorphosed into an archetype or pattern.

Behind all this lies a special metaphysics derived from

that of Plato via Plotinus. That metaphysics assumes the real (i.e., ideal) existence of class-traits. Such a Platonic passage as the speech of Diotima in the *Symposium* gave a philosophic basis for the theory that Beauty is an ideal, absolutely existing like a mathematical circle or triangle or formula above and beyond all its earthly incorporations. It was that which all beautiful objects had in common. This theory is too well-known to require exposition here and we shall not add another inadequate account to those which others have given, especially since none of them equals in power Plato's own exposition. What must, however, be emphasized again is that the theory seemed to imply the obligation of every particular to be a representative of its natural class. Thus a man was admitted to have both generic and individual traits, but it was his duty to turn away from those characteristics which marked him as an individual being and devote himself to those which he had in common with all other men. No one can deny that such a program would make descriptive anthropology much easier, as it would any scientific generalizations. Clearly, if a biologist were to look exclusively at the peculiar individual properties of his frogs and fruit flies, he would never be able to write any laws descriptive of their behaviour in general. But fruit flies and frogs, if they have any interests, cannot make them known. They simply exist and men study them. One might even say that as far as we are concerned, they exist for us, for in any event we overlook any rights they may have to live their own lives. But we men do not exist exclusively in order to make biology, psychology, and anthropology possible. Nor do we live in order to make laws applicable. And consequently we frequently have a feeling that the obligation to conform to the standards of our natural group—*homo sapiens*—is none too compulsive.

7

If there are two kinds of men, those who have been called
centrifugal and those called centripetal, then the psycholo-
gists and their colleagues must make the best of it.
Neither will feel the necessity of turning into the other in
order to get into a treatise on human traits. As for the
pathos of the word " natural," we may even retort to those
who play upon it, that in one of the many senses of that
word, it is characteristic of man to be unnatural. The
Cynics used to maintain that houses, clothing, cooked
food, book-learning, politeness, earning one's living were
not natural; witness the beasts. And indeed, though we
might have been better off in some ways if we had clung
to our caves on the banks of the Vézère, we did not do so.
Nor is it likely that we shall return to them in the future in
order to be more natural.[1]

5. *The natural class of works of art*

It is well known to readers of the *Republic* that Plato
had no high opinion of artisans and poets, and that,
thought he speaks in the *Phaedrus* of beauty's being the
one idea which bridges the gap between the material and
the ideal worlds, he is not speaking of the beauty of works
of art. In fact, there is reason to believe that he would
not have admitted that there were any ideas of artificial
objects at all; ideas being the eternal patterns of natural
objects, the imitation of which is art. Be that as it may,
the aesthetic problem is bound to arise sooner or later of
what is the natural class of a work of art. It was easy
enough for Aristotle with his relatively few objects before
him, the tragedies of a few writers, all written in the same
language about the same themes for the same audience to

---

[1] As a matter of cold fact, we are not our remote ancestors and
hence cannot return.

be produced on the same stage, to make generalizations which would appear reasonable to his readers. But anyone nowadays who would sit down to discover what is common to the tragedies of Shakespeare, Racine, Voltaire, Corneille, Marlowe, Seneca, Euripides and Aeschylus, would soon discover that he had nothing but the common noun, " tragedy," to go on. He may then argue that all these things would not have been called tragedies unless they had something in common, in which case he would show his ignorance of the history of words. It is true that Seneca and Racine deliberately set out to imitate the tragedies of their Greek forebears, and hence their plays do resemble to a certain degree their models. But as far as anyone knows, neither Marlowe nor Shakespeare had any such intention and when one discusses the tragic essence as it appears in *Hamlet,* one can at best mean, Does *Hamlet* resemble, for instance, *Oedipus Rex?* It clearly does, as Voltaire saw, only to a slight degree. But this statement of fact becomes relevant to the question of standards only if one assumes that it ought to and here the word " ought " seems to suggest that it is a tragedy in the same sense that *Oedipus Rex* is a tragedy. But if it were, it would resemble it more closely. Surely it is more intelligent to conclude that the word " tragedy " is ambiguous than to argue that *Hamlet* is a bad tragedy. One might as well argue that the platypus is a bad bird or a bad mammal.

This elementary consideration has not prevented critics from arguing that there is a tragic essence and presumably plays which have been called tragedies somehow or other incorporate that essence. The conclusion in that case is inescapable that *Hamlet* is not a tragedy. That a play which is not a tragedy in this curious meaning of the term is on that account to be disapproved of, seems to be at the least somewhat arbitrary. One might just as well argue that Sophocles should have imitated the primitive tragedies, the goat-songs of the pre-Thespian period. If he and his modern successors had, we should now possess an uninterrupted series of repetitions, copies of copies of copies. But one might also maintain that in order to achieve a more perfect unity, any variation in subject-matter should also be avoided and that one Goat-Song would have sufficed as a perfect specimen of its type to be acted and re-enacted world without end.

No one of course has ever talked such nonsense and most critics of this type have escaped the difficulties of their position by maintaining that tradition grows. So does a human being. And the unity which exists between an adult and the infant which he once was may sometimes be very great, sometimes very small, all depending on where he has lived, with whom he has associated, what books he has read, how much he has traveled. However similar an adult may be to the infant he once was, he is not that infant. And similarly however much *Hamlet* may resemble *Oedipus,* it is not *Oedipus.* This fact must be recognized by anyone who has ever read the two plays and is recognized. The question therefore turns into that of how far a man writing in 1600 may differ from a man writing in 450 B. C. If the two men were one, then a certain degree of difference might be interpreted as insanity. But in the case of plays, neither the plays nor the authors of the plays are the same. Shakespeare is not an older Sophocles except in a very metaphorical sense. He is another person. And the similarity to be found between his plays and those of the Greek dramatists is to be explained on historical, not logical nor metaphysical, grounds.

But there is another approach to this question of what

is the natural class of a work of art. It may arise from prior assumptions about legitimate human purposes. We have for instance none of the Satyr-plays which accompanied the Greek tragedies. They may have died out because of their supposedly obscene character. If so, and such would be a plausible explanation, the time came when the kind of obscenity which some of the Greeks admired was disapproved of. (Even in museums of art, many of the Greek vases are still hidden.) This might be an example of how ethical considerations have killed a type of artistry. Where people for long periods of time, to take the opposite example, have admired a type of art, such as patriotic hymns, it will be preserved and fortified by the inertia of custom and will establish a type which seems to be eternal. What human purposes are legitimate and what not, how persistant are human ends, is a problem for the anthropologist, and it is likely that whatever our purposes, such as the economic and erotic, each society enforces its own standards upon the manner of attaining them. Obscenity has not died out; it has gone underground. Obscene passages in Catullus, Martial, and Ovid are not printed in text-books, but they still exist; similar themes are played upon during the Middle Ages and no demonstration is needed of their existence today. But one does not expect to open a book of lyric poems and find obscenity mixed in with patriotic hymns, odes to skylarks, and laments over the passage of time.

6. *The romantic swing towards particularism*

Since the Romantic Movement, there has been a swing away from Neo-Platonism towards particularism. The reality of variety and change has been admitted in many quarters and the assertion has been made that deviation from the norm is as natural as conformity to it. Being true to oneself, living one's own life, self-expression, have accompanied a kind of nominalism which not only accepts the multiple but admires it. Each work of art is seen to be an individual creation of an individual man; it is *his* work and gains force by its originality and uniqueness. It no longer seems reasonable to urge poets to copy Vergil and Homer or anyone else; painters are not supposed to be latter-day Raphaels; architects no longer have to build Greek temples. A work of art which is little more than a reproduction of another man's work seems of no importance, no matter how beautiful the original may have been. But the constant harping upon originality has led some men to write in an idiom which is next to incomprehensible, painters to paint pictures which critics cannot interpret, composers to write music which sounds like noise to some ears. The situation is that which obtains in the history of a language. Regardless of the work of academies and lexicographers, as well as grammarians, languages change. But the inclination to use one's own idiom is always counter-balanced by the necessity for being intelligible and though Shakespeare needs a glossary today, there is a common fund of identical words and phrases to make him on the whole intelligible.

Moreover, if we are to talk about things, we shall be forced to use common nouns and adjectives, and they will have meaning only if they refer to things which have common properties. And even the Romanticists soon banded together in *petites chapelles* in which they worshipped in common the same gods and demigods. When one goes to an exhibition of contemporary painting, one sees canvases which Bellori, it is true, would not have understood, but they all have certain general traits, certain mannerisms in the use of color, drawing, design, which emerge on closer acquaintance and which have made the public call them modern.

7. *Originality as a standard*

To deviate from the accepted norm is not necessarily to be unclassifiable. A sur-realist who insists that his pictures are his own because they arise unaided by reason from the depths of his Unconscious, is deviating from the tradition of representative painting. But, as psychoanalysts have shown, the Unconscious of two people is more likely to be similar than their Conscious. Hence such paintings will fall into the class of things which are expressions of repressions and when two people are living under the same social conditions, their repressions are usually found to have something in common. Their originality comes out when one compares them with paintings deliberately made according to academic rules. Historically, then, one is deviating from ritualized forms, patterns, ideas, goals; one is not deviating from everything. One may try to escape the limitations of the medium, paint, by making collages of bits of newspaper, twine, tinfoil, photographs, and so on. But even here there is a limit to what odds and ends one can pick up. It is not without interest to find that the early collages were made of the same materials, the things that usually lie about a studio. It is not a hard and fast rule that a collage must contain a bit of newsprint. But old newspapers lie at hand and hence are used. The same observation may be made about the material which appears in many still-lifes and in the flat patterns abstracted from still lifes. The mandoline, the guitar, the bit of peasant pottery, the playing cards, an occasional fruit, are as standardized as the angels and scrolls that float over the heads of holy figures in medieval tapestries. How could it be otherwise? The human imagination is not entirely free. There are limits, as was known in the very beginning of psychology, to the power of invention.

The result is that neither what we have called "the romantic" program of self-assertion and originality, nor that of the traditionalists will stand up under examination. One will in spite of all desire to be original conform to some type of behaviour and hence will find one's originality restrained. If one wishes to be a traditionalist in the purest sense of the term, one will be forced into being a copyist and nothing more. To be original as Théophile Gautier was original is to deviate from the standards of the 1830's. It is not to be unlike anyone who ever existed before or who has existed since. But it is doubtful whether anyone ever pretended to be either so traditionalistic or so original as the theories behind such pretensions would demand. The man of originality usually is simply one who perceives the possibility of new purposes which may be gratified through artistry; the traditionalist simply one who succeeds to his own satisfaction in reinterpreting the works of art of the past in a manner gratifying to a later age. Sometimes, as in the Neo-classic period at the end of the eighteenth century, it was more of a deviation to return to Greece and Rome than to follow one's elder contemporaries. And similarly, as today, few artists are more intolerant of personal deviations from the new academies than the *avant-garde*.

CHAPTER ELEVEN

THE INEFFABLE

WITH ALL of these difficulties, ambiguities, problems of evidence, problems of interpretation behind us, there remains the discouraging fact that in every work of art is an ineffable residue. We do not mean by the word "ineffable" that its object cannot be named, but that it cannot be described. This chapter will consist simply of a list of such things.

1. *Qualities*

By qualities we mean the theoretically simple sensory experiences such as red, green, brown, loud, soft, sweet, bitter, rough and smooth. No one has ever doubted that such things must be felt to be understood. A color-blind man can understand that there is a distinction between red and green but he cannot see it. So a deaf man who can see may be told that there are such things as sounds, corresponding to colors, but again he has no direct experience of them and thus can never know precisely what they are like. We communicate such experiences by naming them to people who have shared them and know the meaning of our names.

2. *Qualities in combination*

Such qualities never come alone, except when a loud explosion is heard, so loud that it occupies the field of our entire attention, or when we are overwhelmed by the blackness of the night, or in some similar situations.

Usually they occur in combination with other qualities. We can name the elements of such combinations and thus tell others what we have experienced. But there are also occasions on which the combination itself has a quality. A chord in music, a melodic phrase, a visual pattern, a short sentence or phrase, have a quality of their own. They are grasped as units and the quality of the unit is not the sum of the qualities of its parts. So the meaning of an idiom is not the sum of the meanings of its component words. The meaning of " What is the matter? " can not be deduced out of the meaning of the word " matter " unless one knows a good bit more of philology than most of us know. In the same way the quality of " It was a beauteous evening calm and free " is in part dependent on the order of the words, not simply on the words, and that order of those words occurs uniquely in this line.

3. *The affective tone of the above*

Since many of our qualitative experiences are either pleasant or unpleasant, and since the peculiar agreeableness of a qualitative experience can not be isolated from the experience itself, the combined quality-and-affective-color becomes a third example of indescribable but possibly nameable experiences. Our names now become less satisfactory however. For the agreeableness of a line of poetry or of a simple visual pattern, such as might be found in a not too elaborate piece of jewelry, or of a subject in a fugue is not merely agreeableness, but the special agreeableness of that particular line or pattern or subject.

4. *Emotional states*

The same remarks apply to our emotional states. We are in the habit of calling these states by specific names, such as anger or fear or delight or anxiety, but when we reflect upon them we see that such names are much too general to do the work that is asked of them. To be angry at an act of insolence is not the same thing as to be angry at one's failure to understand a problem, at brutality to animals or children, at being annoyed or bored. Moreover, a given emotion does not always or even normally attach itself to a given sensory or perceptual experience. Some people, to take an ordinary example, are afraid of dogs, their fear running from blind terror to a mild dislike; others on the contrary not only like dogs, but some go to the point of rapture when they see them. The fear that one has of a dog is not the fear that one has of fire or of drowning; and similarly the pleasure that one has at the sight of a dog is not identical with the pleasure that one has at the sight of an apple tree in bloom. It goes without saying that were there nothing in common in experiences which we call fear or anger or love or hate, they would not have been given the same names. The point which we are trying to make is that there are times when the differences are more important than the similarities. And the emotions aroused in us by works of art illustrate this.

5. *The individual*

Individual people, historical events, things are given proper names. When we speak of George Washington, World War I, *The Decline and Fall of the Roman Empire*, we are not describing anything, we are naming. Each of these things belongs to several classes, but each is a peculiar specimen of the classes to which it belongs and is, moreover, the point at which these classes overlap. When one identifies something by a name, one is saying nothing about its nature. One has simply gummed a label

on it. Herein lies the great difference between what might
be called history and science. Others may use these two
terms differently, but we are pointing out that there is
a discipline which attempts to paint a portrait of individual events and people and families and another which
attempts to discuss groups of things. In so far as works
of art are individuals, and they all are, and in so far as the
critic is interested in what distinguishes the work of art
before him, he cannot be engaged in science. The critic
may be interested, to be sure, in the problem of how far
his work of art resembles other works of art, how far it
conforms to type. In that case he is moving in the direction of science. But when he is interested in how far it
differs from type and in what its individuality consists,
then he approaches the discipline of the historian and
biographer. It perhaps is not necessary to point out that
the scientist cannot deal exclusively with generalities.
Either he or his predecessors have dealt with particulars
at some stage of their development. So the historian does
not deal exclusively with particulars. To the extent that
he uses common nouns and adjectives he will be ap-
proaching the technique of science. Moreover, if he had
the ambition of saying nothing that would be true of anything except the work of art before him, he would be
driven to exhibiting the work of art and saying nothing.

6. *The emotion attached to the work of art as a whole*

As we have hinted above, there is no evidence that anyone has ever grasped as a whole more than a few lines of
poetry or a very small picture or passage of music. Our
perceptions are not synoptic enough to permit us to intuit
longer and larger areas of perception. It is therefore
futile for aestheticians to talk about the unity of works
of art when they are literally speaking of unity of percep-

tion. There may be an overall emotional tone of sadness or gaiety, a feeling of repose or of struggle, but in general more detailed emotional states are as specific as the work of art arousing them. But even when there is emotional unity, it is the emotion-aroused-by-that-specific-work-of-art-on-that-specific-occasion which is in question, nor is there any reason to believe that there is any particular aesthetic emotion which is common to the intuition of all works of art. It is granted that the emotion aroused by a representative work of art is not the same as the emotion aroused by the perception of what it represents. That is, the feelings which one has on seeing a murder on the stage are not the same as the emotion one has on seeing a murder in real life. We are happy to concede the effect of aesthetic distance. But it is precisely this singularity of feeling which has proved the great stumbling block to all monistic and Platonistic theories of aesthetics. It is also this singularity of feeling which accounts for the hopeless diversities in taste, since emotions vary from person to person, to a degree even greater than that of variations in perception. It is moreover this singularity of feeling which is the apology for impressionistic criticism, explains in part the phenomenon of multivalence, and renders impotent the program of prescriptive aesthetics. One cannot legislate man's emotions, though one can force people to lie about them and be hypocritical.

The critic therefore, if he is wise, will confine himself to explanation, interpretation, analysis and give up praising and blaming, legislation, evaluation. He will cease the attempt to communicate the ineffable and resign himself to a world in which there is an insoluble residuum of irrationality.

IL FAUT ETRE DE SON TEMPS [1]

Reprinted by permission of the *Journal of Aesthetics*

ONE of the most important slogans of the French romantic philosophers and artists forms the title of this paper. It is almost the only recorded word of Daumier, for instance, which is left to us, forming, as it were, his heraldic device.[2] It is the burden of the famous *Préface des études françaises et étrangères* of Emile Deschamps.[3] The practice of new metres, styles, techniques, and subject matters, which would appear to be a consequence of its adoption as a program, is a characteristic of French arts in the first half of the nineteenth century. Elaborated into a theory by Deschamps, it had even been given a special name, *helikiasticism,* by an Italian jurist and literary critic, Romagnosi.[4]

[1] The author's debt to the work of Professor A. O. Lovejoy will be apparent to all students of the history of ideas. It requires special acknowledgment, however, since reference cannot be made in footnotes to private conversations.

[2] See the frontispiece of Arsène Alexandre's *Honoré Daumier, l'Homme et l'Oeuvre,* Paris, 1888. Hereafter French publications will be understood to have been issued in Paris, unless otherwise noted.

[3] Ed. of Henri Girard, in the Bibliothèque romantique, [1923], *passim,* but esp. p. 17.

[4] The place of Romagnosi in Italian romanticism is discussed at length in G. A. Borgese, *Storia della critica romantica in Italia,* Milan 1920, ch. vi. Romagnosi's term first appeared in the *Conciliatore,* no.

To argue that artists should be of their time presupposed the notion that there were such things as *times;* that history was divided into epochs which differed from one another not in superficial traits, such as costume—although even this was not apparently always known—and language, but in such fundamental matters as ways of thinking and evaluating. Such a notion is of course as old as recorded occidental literature, for the legend of the ages is a theory of epochs, if we take the word " theory " loosely enough. Whether this theory was primitivistic or anti-primitivistic, it maintained that human nature varied in time and varied to so deep an extent that men of one age would reverse the moral judgments of another. The influence of Plato and Aristotle with their emphasis upon the universal, of Stoicism with its belief in cosmopolitanism, of Christianity with its acceptance and extension of both, must have been to make men lose sight of temporal as well as of geographical differences, and even when writers belonging to these traditions used the old familiar metaphors or played upon the degeneration of man and nature, as was common in patristic authors,[5] it was in order to insist that the *true,* the best character of man had appeared in one of the epochs, whereas in the others he had lived a monstrous, corrupted, or perverse life.

There is no need in this paper of tracing the history of the idea of epochs as the Romanticists used it. But we

3, p. 11, according to Borgese, *op. cit.*, p. 135, n. l. See also Paul van Tieghem, *Le Mouvement romantique,* 1923, p. 103. On the *Conciliatore,* see Kent Roberts Greenfield, *Economics and Liberalism in the Risorgimento,* Baltimore, The Johns Hopkins Press, 1934, pp. 161 ff.

[5] See, for instance, Lactantius, *Div. inst.*, II, 5, V, 6; St. Ambrose, *Hexameron,* III, x; St. Augustine, *Civ. dei,* Blk. XIII (ch. 20, 21; XV, 9, among others.

may at least suggest some of the earlier phases of the idea in pre-romantic thought. Of these, two are the most important, that to be found in Vico's *Scienza Nuova*, according to which man's whole " spiritual " life varies from age to age—his feeling of justice, beauty, truth, and goodness—and that found as early as Turgot and which developed into Comte's law of the three stages, according to which the thinking processes of men were a function of the period in which they lived.[6] If men think differently according to the period in which they are born and if their judgments of goodness and beauty vary similarly, the whole question of the validity of universal values immediately arises. One could argue (1) that the variation consists either in degeneration or progress or some combination of the two, cyclical or undulatory, or (2) that there was no inherent rightness in any of the periods, but that man's whole spiritual life was determined by what has sometimes been called the *Zeitgeist* and that there was no criterion by which the *Zeitgeist's* variations could be judged. The two points of view are not only logically different, but the psychological attitude presumably associated with them might very well be opposed. Thus a man who believed in undeviating progress towards the

---

[6] *Principii d'una scienza nuova* was first published in 1725 and republished in a highly revised edition in 1730. It was translated into French by Michelet in 1827. Turgot's version of the law of the three stages was first pronounced in a speech on universal history given in 1750, but not published until 1808. I have sketched its history through Condorcet, Saint-Simon, and Comte in my *French Philosophies of the Romantic Period*, Baltimore, The Johns Hopkins Press, 1925, pp. 265 ff. Such theories must not be confused with theories like that of Mme de Stael in her *De la littérature considérée dans ses rapports avec les institutions sociales*. She too believed that literature changed, but as a function of social—by which she usually meant political—institutions.

better would maintain that his period was the best period
so far, but that its goodness consisted in its attainment to
a certain degree of a universal end whose inherent value
would be even greater. Psychologically he might feel that
his duty was to improve his time with the universal end
in mind. The extreme *helikiastic* would refuse to judge
his time by any other, past or future, and would naturally
attempt to discover its peculiarities and to give them what
is usually called " aesthetic expression."

The second was the attitude of the predominant French
romanticists. They were not always consistent about it
nor even clear in their intentions. But on the whole the
preface of Emile Deschamps maintains that regardless of
what other times have been, it is the duty of writers to be
of their own time *avant tout et en tout*. Since this preface
appeared in 1828, it becomes chronologically at any rate
part of a movement to which Comte's law of the three
stages (first published in 1825) [7] and Vico's *Scienza Nuova*
in Michelet's translation gave added impetus.

Michelet's version of Vico's masterpiece, which greatly
abbreviated the original work, was the source of Vico's
influence in France during the second quarter of the nineteenth century. A reader of this book would have found
Vico's theses presented simply and clearly, in a termin-
ology which would have seemed less barbarous than that
of the original. He would have seen in Michelet's introduction the division of history into three periods, the
divine or theocratic, the heroic, the civilized, and the
doctrine that the differences between the periods was
most clearly marked by the type of language which they

[7] In " Considérations philosophiques sur les sciences et les savans,"
Producteur, 1825, Vol. I, 289. Comte maintained that he " discovered " the law in 1822.

spoke.[8] The Heroic Age spoke a metaphorical and poetic language, the Theocratic *une langue hiéroglyphique ou sacrée.* It would thus have been impossible for a man not to be of his epoch, for epochs were homogeneous.[9] As for Deschamps, he was convinced that the importance of the romantic movement in literature lay in its sponsorship of modern art as distinguished from the art of the past. He emphasized in his famous preface " two great truths,"

qu'il n'y a réellement pas de romantisme, mais bien une littérature du dix-neuvième siècle; et en second lieu, qu'il n'existe dans ce siècle, comme dans tous, que de bons et de mauvais ouvrages, et même, si vous voulez, infiniment plus de mauvais que de bons.[9]

The first truth was not open to discussion, if words were taken in their literal meaning. The second immediately opened the question of the criterion of good literature. In what sense of the word could a book written in the nineteenth century be bad? The answer would be simply that bad literature was literature that imitated the work of another century. The writer must always strive for novelty.

Les hommes d'un vrai talent de chaque époque sont toujours doués d'un instinct qui les pousse vers le nouveau.[10]

But here again a number of questions arise, of which two are outstanding: (1) Is there anything besides chronology which defines an epoch; (2) could not novelty consist precisely in imitating or reviving a previous style? If,

[8] *Principes de la Philosophie de l'histoire,* 1827, p. xvii.

[9] Similar thoughts stimulated by a reading of Vico, were to be found in the Traditionalists, Bonald and Maistre. In fact, they were a commonplace of Catholic writers. See Elio Gianturco, *Joseph de Maistre and Giambattista Vico,* Washington, 1937.

[9a] *Ed. cit.,* p. 6.

[10] *Id.,* p. 7.

that is, literature of the nineteenth century is simply literature written between 1800 and 1900, is not literature
which continues the tradition of earlier periods but which
is written between these two dates as much a part of the
total body of nineteenth century art as a selected portion
of that literature? In the second place, was it not peculiar
to the early nineteenth century to attempt the revival of
Roman, if not Greek styles? Much of the work of David,
Canova, Delille, Ingres, Huvé, perhaps Spontini also, succeeded in establishing an artistic style which even with our
perspective we see as peculiar to its time.

We do not know whether Deschamps ever seriously
considered these questions. He was writing polemics, not
history, and he was trying to justify the artistic practices
of a group of his contemporaries who were producing
relatively novel works of art. His argument ran, French
poetry is strong in philosophical epistles, didactic poems
and fables; it is weak in the epic, the lyric, the elegiac.
Therefore men who write the former run after *des palmes
déjà cueillies;* it is no longer possible to write masterpieces
in these fields which are encumbered with them.[11] But in
the latter field there is still room and it is in that field that
Deschamps' friends, Hugo, Lamartine, and Vigny, were
working. The fact that they were producing new forms of
French poetry ought to have sufficed to justify them in his
eyes. But Deschamps, unhappily for logic, utilizes other
criteria of greatness, as when he praises Hugo's odes for
their lack of false ornament, cold exclamation, *en-
thousiasme symétrique,* and for the presence in them of
" all the secrets of the heart, all the dreams of the imagination, and all the sublimity of philosophy." [12]

If one went then to the most influential manifesto of the

[11] *Id.,* p. 9.   [12] *Id.,* p. 13 f.

Romanticists to find out what a " time " was, one would be disappointed. It is easy enough by running through the periodical literature of the Restoration to find a copious supply of paragraphs emphasizing the differences between epochs, the necessity of being modern, the need for originality, but if one seek a clear definition of a period and a receipt for belonging to a period, the search will be vain.

There was, however, another element in the idea which must not be overlooked. That was the opposition to something known as " ideal beauty." This opposition appears among those who might be called theoretical writers in a very pronounced form in Stendhal. We all know the influence which the Idéologues and their theory of the analysis of ideas had upon him and how much of his literary technique is an application of ideological analysis. His hatred of the " empty ideas of Plato, Kant, and their school," [13] was never reticent. This expresses itself more forcibly in the life of Rossini, the letters on Haydn, and in his history of painting.[14] But Delacroix, too, who was no great admirer of Stendhal at least in the twenties,[15] resents the idea of unchanging and absolute beauty. In 1823 or 1824 he writes,

[13] *Promenades dans Rome*, 1829, I, 241. Cf. Garat on the German infatuation with the *idées platoniques de Mendelssohn* and his school in the *Conservateur*, no. 50, 29 vendémiaire VI (20 Oct. 1797), p. 396.

[14] *Vie de Rossini*, ed. Champion, 1923, p. 17: *le beau idéal* change *tous les trente ans en musique*; *Lettres sur Haydn*, same edition, 1914, Letter XIX and reply, esp. pp. 209 ff.; *Histoire de la Peinture en Italie*, same edition, 1924, I, 133 . Cf. H. Delacroix's *Psychologie de Stendhal*, 1918, pp. 213 ff.

[15] See his Journal, under 25 January 1824, after reading Stendhal on Rossini.

La question sur le beau se réduit à peu près à ceci: Qu'aimez-vous mieux d'un lion ou d'un tigre? Un Grec et an Anglais ont chacun une façon d'être beau qui n'a rien de commun.[16]

In fact, the idea of the varieties of beauty ran constantly through his mind and we find one of his rare theoretical writings given over entirely to that subject.[17] Though he attacks originality and novelty, (15 May 1824), he also attacks copying and imitation.[18] But more influential than such almost unknown pronouncements must have been Daumier's caricatures, whose burdens during the forties were the ugliness of the nude human body, a subject dear to believers in ideal beauty, and the absurdity of the French classical drama. These two series of caricatures would have sufficed to make what the classicists called ideal beauty an object of ridicule.[19] Given their date, these drawings could not have initiated the campaign against the ideal, but they were the strongest kind of propaganda in orienting the public mind against it.

No one in the nature of things could have told what ideal beauty was. And consequently in practice its pur-

---

[16] *Journal*, 1826, I, 47.

[17] "Variations du beau," *Revue des Deux Mondes*, 15 July 1857. Cf. his "Questions sur le Beau," Id. 15 July 1854.

[18] 1834, no date, *Journal*, I, 194. It should not be forgotten that as Delacroix grew older, his ideas on many subjects changed. To take but one example, and that a very striking one, he said in May 1824 that he could paint only when his *esprit brouillon s'agite, défasse, essaye de cent manières, avant d'arriver au but dont le besoin me travaille dans chaque chose.* . . . *Si je ne suis pas agité comme un serpent dans la main d'une pythonisse, je suis froid; il faut le reconnaître et s'y soumettre. Tout se que j'ai fait de bien a été fait ainsi.* But on April 7, 1849 he writes, *L'art n'est plus alors ce que croit le vulgaire, c'est-à-dire une sorte d'inspiration qui vient de je ne sais où, etc.*

[19] See especially the *Baigneurs* (1842), the *Physionomies tragico-classiques* (1841) and the *Physionomies tragiques* (1851).

suit meant the following of certain academic rules regarding subject matter and technique in vogue in the academies and exemplified by the established artists of the late eighteenth century. David apparently knew the rules in painting as Delille did in poetry. To be of one's time therefore meant in effect to write poetry which was not like that of Delille and to paint pictures which were not like those of David. It is a commonplace of the history of art that the subject matter of David was classical, in the sense of its being chosen from Greek and Roman mythology and history, and that his technique was classical in subordinating color to sculpturesque form and in calm and well-balanced compositions. Similar remarks could be made about literature: J-B. Rousseau, Lebrun, Bertin, Parny were polished and facile writers, but they lacked what Deschamps called inspiration and greatness. With their imitations of Greek and Latin pastorals, they avoided contemporary subjects unless they could present them in allegorical form. Such men painted pictures and wrote books which exemplified the rules.

It was the revolt against the rules—which in actual practice meant the departure from the habitual—which seemed to annoy the critics of romanticism the most. It was the defence of romantic departure from the rules, from "correctness," which occupied the last part of Deschamp's preface. The defence rested mainly upon the thesis that there simply was no correct way of writing which would be correct for every subject and, what is more important, for every man. *Autant d'hommes de talent, autant de styles.*[20] But again, Deschamps gives us no clue as to how he would discover a man of talent. A man without talent, however, is more simply defined; he is a man who writes *comme tout le monde.*

[20] Op. cit., p. 58.

If artists of the romantic period wished to find originality, they could do it in two ways, by seeking new subject matters and by developing new techniques. Among the former were scenes from contemporary life, emphasis upon national tradition as distinguished from Pagan tradition, painting scenes from Christian rather than from Greek and Roman history and hence Gothic rather than Classical themes, emphasizing color more than line and form. Each of these items when developed became an artistic creed in the nineteenth century. Peasant life, urban life, the ugly, all provided material for the new artists. Since one must be original, one must experiment, and the artist quickly grew as convinced as the scientist of the truth of the proposition that all truth was not as yet discovered. That was perhaps one of the most fundamental changes in outlook which nineteenth century artists had to face. For when they believed in eternal beauty, it was simple enough to believe that there were eternal rules for achieving it. Just as the believers in eternal truth spent their time expounding it rather than in experimenting, so believers in eternal beauty spent theirs in reproducing it. But as soon as the notion gained ground that beauty was something which changed from epoch to epoch, there was no reason why the rules for achieving it should not change as rapidly.

The problem facing philosophers of art accordingly became that of determining what the modern epoch " really " was. It does not take deep reflection to see that every epoch is by nature complex. When one passes beyond the limitations of Australian bush-society—if the usual accounts of that society be true—when labor becomes specialized, different interests are bound to arise and the question of which interest or set of interests " really " typifies the society arises also. We are fortunately not called upon to discuss the validity of the answers; we need simply indicate them.

Such terms as " pastoral," " military," " theocratic," " heroic," when applied to societies and epochs apparently mean—when interpreted most charitably—that the controlling forces in the societies and epochs so named could most fittingly be qualified by such adjectives. To call a society " pastoral " could no more mean that everyone in it was a shepherd than the term " heroic " could mean that everyone living in heroic society was a hero. For our purposes, it is important to know what the thinkers of the early nineteenth century, whether " romantic " or not, thought was the dominant character of their time and nothing more. Nor shall we list all the various opinions of that period, but confine ourselves to the most important examples.

As one goes through the literature the following points of view appear among the more prominent.

1. *Nineteenth century society was a return to the Catholic royalism of the Capetian dynasty.*

This was the opinion of the so-called Traditionalists, among the most prominent of whom was the Vicomte de Bonald. Authority, tradition, good taste, the principles of eternal beauty, were among their most frequently repeated phrases. This group was the nucleus of the famous Société des Bonnes Lettres, which was an organization of Parisian aristocracy, including at its start Chenedollé, Victor Hugo, Lamartine, Charles Nodier, and Alfred de Vigny, though later most of these men became leaders of the aesthetic opposition.[21] The affiliation of the antiromanticists with royalism is best illustrated by two

[21] This is from the list of members for 1826. See Ch.-M. des Granges, *Le romantisme et la critique*, 1907, p. 197.

selections from articles which appeared in the *Annales de la littérature et des arts* (Vol. XX, 1825, p. 501).

Qu'est-ce que le romantique? C'est, il me semble, l'indépendance de toutes les règles et autorités consacrées: c'est tantôt l'imitation exacte d'une nature brute et sans choix, tantôt l'expression recherchée d'une nature fantastique; c'est l'alliance de l'ignoble et du maniéré, du buffon et de l'ampoulé. En un mot, c'est l'absence de goût.[22]

This in itself would not be an expression of royalism, but when it is coupled with the following, the intention becomes clearer.

Ecrivains royalistes, coeurs pleins de loyauté, pleins de flamme, espoir d'une littérature illustrée par des noms si fameux, gardez-vous de prendre un étendard différent du nôtre, quand nous combattons d'une même ardeur les doctrines impies, les fureurs révolutionnaires. Tout blasphème contre Racine ou Fénelon vous irrite, sans doute, autant qu'une diatribe contre Henri IV ou Louis XIV, car tout se lie dans les sentiments royalistes; ainsi que les éloquents auteurs du *Génie du Christianisme, De la Législation primitive* et de *l'Essai sur l'indifférence*, marchons au combat, précédés par les images de nos pères.[23]

2. *The nineteenth century was the reconciliation between the spirit of revolution and that of royalism, between authority and individual reason.*

This was the point of view of Cousin and the eclectic school in general, the philosophy of the *juste milieu*. A contemporary of Cousin describes the early years of the Restoration in the following words.

Quel tableau que celui des années 1816 et 1817! l'ordonnance du 5 septembre, la chambre de salut contre la contre-révolution, la loi des

---

[22] Quoted by Des Granges, *op. cit.*, pp. 192 f. Cf. Alexis Dumesnil, *Histoire de l'esprit public en France depuis 1789*, 1840, p. 122 f.

[23] From the *Annales*, XIII, 1823, p. 415; quoted by Des Granges, *op. cit.*, p. 206. Cf. Des Granges, pp. 187 ff., 194, 214, 225.

élections, la loi de recrutement, la loi sur la presse; la tribune devenue, d'un premier élan, rivale de la tribune anglaise, d'une splendeur de parole dégagée du théâtral de la révolution, mais gardant l'essor vers le beau en même temps que vers le vrai; tous les partis armés de foi, de verve et d'éloquence, toutes les plumes aiguisées et alertes au combat; la *Minerve* libérale, le *Conservateur* royaliste, les *Archives* doctrinaires; et au-dessous, je ne sais combien de journaux inexpéri-mentés, mais sincères quoi qu'on en ait dit; ici, de bonapartistes de la veille, se réveillant malgré eux libéraux par nécessité de défaite et de défense d'abord, puis par reflexion et conviction acquise au combat; là, de royalistes, hier encore absolutistes, forcés aussi, comme les vaincus qu'ils foulaient aux pieds, de se réfugier dans la liberté, leur grand tribun en tête qui leur jetait dans la *Monarchie selon la Charte* un livre de Montesquieu! [24]

This picture of a society in which the most extreme elements were brought together in a kind of legal freedom may have been composed after reflection rather than upon observation. But in any event it presents one with the kind of picture which the leader of the Eclectics, Victor Cousin, would have admired. For above all things he stood for something which he called " reconciliation " and he no doubt honestly believed that reconciliation was a synthesis of antithetical characters. It was in that spirit that the *Globe*, which tried to be fair to all parties, in-sisted that romanticism was not the name of a *genre* and that the romanticists were as much in disagreement over their policies as the classicists.[25] Cousin thought that his philosophy was an expression of the same spirit as that introduced into literature by Chateaubriand and Mme de

[24] Paul Dubois, *Cousin, Jouffroy, Damiron, Souvenirs*, 1902, pp. 40 ff.

[25] See *Du Romantique* signed " O," [Duvergier de Hauranne?] in the *Globe* of March 24, 1825, p. 423.

Stael,[26] and both Stendhal and Deschamps wrote of him as the spokesman of their contemporaries.[27]

But for Cousin ideal beauty was far from being an illusion. It was in fact the one reality, identical in substance with the true and the good. All the mysticism of Plotinus and Schelling was expressed in his enthusiasm for the ideal. And when he came to appreciate works of art, we find him a fervent admirer of the French seventeenth century: Corneille, Racine, Boileau, Lesueur, Poussin, Claude, in fact all the great and solemn masters of the age of Louis XIV. There was little here upon which a new aesthetics could be founded.

3. *The nineteenth century was the age of positivistic science, observation of facts, not explanation of causes, industrial organization, the domination of society by economic forces.*

This was in particular the theory of Comte, but was of course shared in varying degrees by Saint-Simon and Proudhon. Comte believed that when the nineteenth century really fulfilled itself, there would be a ruling class which would direct the work of artists as well as of scientists. The true aim of art for Comte was " to charm and ameliorate humanity," [20] and that aim could only be accomplished by strengthening the social order. When one asked who would determine what strengthened and what weakened the social order, the answer was clearly the political rulers of society.

Whatever French artists may have thought about the

[26] *Du Vrai, du Beau, du Bien*, iii.

[27] Stendhal in *Racine et Shakespeare*, ch. vii; Deschamps in *op. cit.*, p. 25.

[28] *Politique positive*, Vol. I, p. 280. Cr. *French Philosophies of the Romantic Period*, pp. 296 ff.

purpose of their art, it is obvious that the new subject matters were as they would have been if the artists had believed in the doctrines of Comte. Daumier is a special case, since his craft was that of a caricaturist and his political beliefs were of the opposition. But even in artists who had no political bias as artists, men like the members of the Barbizon School, there was a turning away from scenes of court life, from Pagan history and mythology, from illustration to classical drama. One is not a positivist for painting peasants, but when artists began to paint peasants seriously, without idealization, it became possible for positivists to see their work as the glorification of labor. So when Courbet later painted nudes which did not illustrate the canon of human proportion as taught in the academies, it was possible for Proudhon to interpret them as satires of the bourgeoisie, " deformed by fat and rich living." [29] It should be understood by now that no work of art is univalent. But of all works of art, pictures, because of their having usually a subject matter which may be interpreted either literally or figuratively, are most likely to be invested with a multiplicity of values. Thus regardless of what Courbet may have intended to put into his *Baigneuses*, Proudhon found in it a social document, a commentary on a social class with a " message " which he was undoubtedly free to interpret as he would. And it was largely through the interpretation of nineteenth century paintings, and not through the subject matters as seen by angels removed from space and time, that an artist became of his time.

It is clear that the nineteenth century was not only an industrial century, it was also a century of constitutional monarchy and of Catholic royalism. It was a century of democratic progress, a century of imperialistic exploita-

[29] *Du principe de l'art et de sa destination sociale*, 1865, p. 287.

tion, a century of scientific exploration, in fact, a century
of whatever a commentator felt to be its most important
innovation—and there was a large choice. For no time is
simple, but all would appear to be highly complex tissues
of conflicting and harmonious tendencies. In the history
of ideas and of institutions one finds three phenomena at
all times; the retention of certain traditions, the revival—
deliberate or accidental, conscious or unconscious—of
antiquity, the development of what was merely inchoate
in previous times. Thus in the early nineteenth century
in France, one finds the retention of French classical traditions in art, as in Ingres and his school, the revival of the
Gothic, and the development of what might be called the
" sentimentalism " of Rousseau. No one of these details
is the complete picture of the time—nor are all three—
but it is precisely in the peculiar combination of various—
and sometimes conflicting—tendencies that the time is
characterized.

It is for that reason that when one goes back to the
twenties and thirties of the last century and tries to select
the Frenchmen who most perfectly symbolize the romantic
movement for us, one thinks of Delacroix, Hugo, Berlioz,
and possibly Viollet-le-Duc. Yet if we read the journals
of these men we find that their respect for one another
was frequently very slight. Delacroix loathed the music
of Berlioz (who in turn loathed that of Rossini). He
particularly admired the paintings of Meissonier, of whom
he said, " Après tout, de nous tous, c'est lui qui est le plus
sûr de vivre." [30] Yet no one would think today of classify-
ing Meissonier in the same group with Géricault and Delacroix. His opinion of Hugo was as low as Hugo's opinion

---

[30] Quoted by Baudelaire in his famous letter on Delacroix in the
Opinion Nationale. See his *Oeuvres complètes,* ed. F.-F. Gautier, Vol.
IV (*l'Art Romantique*), 1923, p. 194.

of him.[31] And the only time Viollet-le-Duc is mentioned in his journal is when he includes him in a list of guests at a dinner party (July 31, 1855). Delacroix was not the whole romantic movement, to be sure, nor can he speak for all, but a student would find that his attitude towards his fellow romantics is not unusual.

To be of one's time is a task which one fulfills through the fatality of one's dates. Artists make their time as other people do and the notion that there is a time external to the events which take place in it requires but a little reflection to be discredited. What the aestheticians of the early nineteenth century wanted was some justification for being different from their predecessors. Why they should have wanted to be different is not explained by their dates alone; all artists—as the history of art shows—have been different from their predecessors. But in the early nineteenth century the whole structure of French society, political as well as ideological, had changed, and men no doubt felt uneasy in repeating ideas and making gestures which seemed more appropriate to a previous society. The break between revolutionary France and royalist France was one which was profoundly felt in all ranks of society and in all fields of human activity. Times had not only changed but every one was aware of the changes that had taken place. The Restoration was an attempt to return to the age of Louis XIV, as the Empire was an attempt to return to that of Augustus Caesar. Both attempts now seem like complete failures. But the writers and other artists of that period saw the difference between their epoch and previous epochs. That does not mean that they were able either to understand or even to define in what the difference lay. Nor need we, reading their books and looking at their pictures, feel that we see in them what their creators saw.

[31] See Delacroix's *Journal*, ed. cit., I, 210 and note.

THE MONA LISA IN THE HISTORY OF TASTE

Reprinted from *Journal of the History of Ideas*, April, 1940, Vol. I, No. 2, pages 207-224.

THE SEARCH for aesthetic standards by means of which any work of art can be finally judged would seem to presuppose either that every such work is an unchanging entity, or that, regardless of whether it changes or not, it should always be judged in the same way. Neither of these presuppositions appears tenable to the writer of this paper, who holds, on the contrary, that works of art are not the locus of one value, known as " beauty " or something similar, but are rather multivalent, that certain of their values are experienced by some persons, others by others, and that there is no *a priori* method—except that of fiat—of determining which of the many values are properly " aesthetic." One objection usually raised against this position is that there happen to be some works of art which " the judgment of posterity " has always held to be admirable or " great," and that one has only to examine their characteristics to discover what the distinguishing marks of great works of art are. The Parthenon, the *Aeneid, Hamlet,* and so on, it is maintained, have always enjoyed a high reputation. They are great by almost universal consent; or, if there have been periods when they were not highly esteemed, that is because the people of those periods had poor taste.

It cannot be denied that there are works of art which have almost always been greatly admired. (For the sake of the argument one may neglect those times when they were not discussed at all, having been overlooked for some reason or other.) But having admitted that, one faces the question whether the name, *Hamlet*, or the Parthenon, or the *Aeneid*, has always meant the same thing. Physically, the words or the shapes of stone in which they are embodied have changed little, though the little is not without some importance; but the physical basis of these and other works of art is only a small part of them. More important is what people have looked for in them and either found or not found. Thus the *Aeneid* as a Roman epic differs from the *Aeneid* as an instrument of magic, and *Hamlet* as a chivalric tragedy of revenge differs from *Hamlet* as a Freudian drama. It may be argued that the work of art as the artist intended it is the real work of art, and that we should suspend judgment until we have recaptured it in its primitive state. In most cases such a quest is probably futile, for we often have no way of knowing what an artist intended, and in any event we can, for the most part, only reconstruct what he intended from what we ourselves find. And that is to no small extent dependent upon our education and our original nature. Moreover, to recapture through study an artist's intention is different from reacting directly to a work of art; and the professor of English literature who, having studied Elizabethan language and customs and theatrical practice and the biography of Shakespeare, reads *Hamlet*, is not psychologically identical with the Elizabethan spectator who went to the theater and saw *Hamlet* during what might be called its lifetime. Whatever else Shakespeare may have been up to, he was certainly not producing plays for professors of English to study three hundred years after his death. We may reasonably conclude that to define the work of art as the work intended by the artist gives us only the slenderest clues to appropriate standards for judging it.

The purpose of this paper is to take one of the works of art which have been most admired until recent times, and to examine briefly what critics or commentators of different periods have said about it. From what they said we hope to be able to infer what they were looking for. We are not so much interested in knowing why they admired the work of art as in knowing what they saw in it. It will be found that in at least this one case the work of art was identical with itself throughout history in name only. We have chosen as our example Leonardo's *Mona Lisa*.

I

The *Mona Lisa*, it should be recalled, is usually considered to be a portrait of the wife of Francesco del Giocondo, painted between 1503 and 1506. There is no conclusive evidence that it was intended as an allegory, though the background does not put that beyond the bounds of possibility.[1] No mention is made of it in the artist's literary remains, so that we do not know at what the artist himself was aiming. We do, however, know what he thought the proper fashion of representing women was, and that will be pointed out later.

Leonardo's contemporaries apparently did not consider

[1] Everything about this famous picture has been disputed. We have accepted the traditional name of the sitter, but A. Venturi in the *Enciclopedia Italiana* maintains that she was Costanza d'Avalos and that the misty background did have allegorical significance. See his section in the article on Leonardo. L. Roger-Milès, in his *Léonard de Vinci et les Jocondes*, 1923, pp. 68 ff., maintains that it is not even a portrait.

8

the *Mona Lisa* his most important work. Several accounts of Italian painting, written during Leonardo's life or a little later, fail even to mention it. This is true of *Il Libro di Antonio Billi* [2] and of an anoymous work written during the forties of the sixteenth century.[3] Paolo Giovio, writing after Leonardo's death, says simply that he painted the portrait of Mona Lisa, " wife of Francesco del Giocondo, which was bought by King Francis I, it is said, for 4000 *scudi*." [4] In the short *Vita* he mentions the *Last Supper* and tells the story of Louis XII's desire to cut it out of the wall on which it was painted, and the *Virgin and Saint Anne*, but does not mention the *Mona Lisa*. There is nothing here, except the unusually high price, which is of interest. The same may be said of the comment of Raffaelo Borghini, made in 1584, that the portrait was such *che non puo l'arte far davantaggio*.[5] More to the point is the criticism of Lomazzo, who praises it along with portraits by Raphael and Andrea del Sarto as peculiarly adapted to its subject.[6]

The most influential of the earlier comments on the *Mona Lisa* is that of Vasari, which established a tradition. This paragraph is the best known of the classical statements, and it was apparently the source of most of the anecdotes repeated in later times about the picture. It was first published in 1550, some forty-odd years after the portrait was painted. The passage runs as follows:

[2] See de Fabriczy, *Arch. Stor. Ital.*, ser. V, tom. 7.

[3] *Ibid.*

[4] See Tiraboschi, *Stor. della lett. Ital.*, T. VI, p. iv, lib. iii, c. 7, xxxii (Venice, 1823, VI, 4-5, p. 1602).

[5] See *Il Riposo*, Florence, 1584, p. 370 f.

[6] G. P. Lomazzo, *Trattato dell' arte della pittura*, etc., Milan, 1584-85, p. 434.

Whoever shall desire to see how far art can imitate nature, may do so to perfection in this head, wherein every peculiarity that could be depicted by the utmost subtlety of the pencil has been faithfully reproduced. The eyes have the lustrous brightness and moisture which is seen in life, and around them are those pale, red, and slightly livid circles, also proper to nature, with the lashes, which can only be copied as they are with the greatest difficulty; the eyebrows also are represented with the closest exactitude, where fuller and where more thinly set, with the separate hairs delineated as they issue from the skin, every turn being followed, and all the pores exhibited in a manner that could not be more natural than it is: the nose, with its beautiful and delicately roseate nostrils, might be easily believed to be alive; the mouth, admirable in its outline, has the lips uniting the rose-tints of their colour with that of the face, in the utmost perfection, and the carnation of the cheek does not appear to be painted, but truly of flesh and blood: he who looks earnestly at the pit of the throat cannot but believe that he sees the beating of the pulses, and it may be truly said that this work is painted in a manner well calculated to make the boldest master tremble, and astonishes all who behold it, however well accustomed to the marvels of art. Mona Lisa was exceedingly beautiful, and while Leonardo was painting her portrait, he took the precaution of keeping some one constantly near her, to sing or play on instruments, or to jest and otherwise amuse her, to the end that she might continue cheerful, and so that her face might not exhibit the melancholy expression often imparted by painters to the likenesses they take. In this portrait of Leonardo's on the contrary there is so pleasing an expression, and a smile so sweet, that while looking at it one thinks it rather divine than human, and it has ever been esteemed a wonderful work, since life itself could exhibit no other appearance.[7]

There are two important features in this criticism: first, it is Leonardo's skill that is the subject of admiration,

[7] Giorgio Vasari, *Lives of the Most Eminent Painters, Sculptors, and Architects*, tr. by Mrs. Jonathan Foster, London, 1876, II, p. 384 f. It is perhaps worth noting that in the eighteenth century Leonardo was to be blamed by at least one writer for too great fidelity to nature, uncorrected by a study of the antique. See [Dezallier d'Argenville,] *Abrégé de la Vie des plus Fameux Peintres*, 1745, p. 74.

rather than the effect of the picture upon the observer, or the " self-expression " of the artist, or a symbol of something called " the times "; second, the painter's skill is supposed to be directed towards reproducing a natural object as faithfully as possible.

To think of the artist as a craftsman who learns and applies a technique is, of course, not unusual in the history of criticism. Even the most fervent admirer of Croce would admit that some artists are more skillful technicians than others. But to focus one's appreciation upon this has been by no means a universal practice among critics. Forgetting, for the purposes of this paper, the past history of such an attitude, as seen, for instance, in the elder Pliny, it is not improbable that technical skill became particularly interesting in the Renaissance, when *homo faber* began experimenting and inventing as he had not done since Alexandrian days.

But one may praise an artist's skill and yet not believe that it was oriented towards a reproduction of " nature." One may admire the exquisite technique of an Odilon Redon, for instance, or a Braque, and say nothing whatsoever about the likeness of its result to anything natural. One may admire the technique of a Byzantine fresco in which the " natural " is almost completely recreated and transformed. The idea that " nature " was of interest and importance in her own right belongs to a period in which men seek to observe facts and record them, and think that observation and record are good in themselves. Vasari, who was himself a painter, is perhaps more sensitive to technical excellence than a critic who has no experience in producing works of art. His own paintings are, like those of most of his contemporaries, admirably skillful in perspective ond other tricks of illusion. It is therefore possible, though not probable, that he was simply erecting his own type of skill into a standard for all artists.

It would, however, be sheer pedantry to attempt to prove what everyone knows, namely, that the Renaissance in Italy was marked by an almost religious regard for what later became natural science, and by a delight in the arts which helped man understand the things of nature.[8] The whole matter has been clearly and succinctly told by Burckhardt in his *The Civilization of the Renaissance in Italy*, and requires no retelling. But it may be said that the Italians of this period were the first men to rediscover natural beauty, to write biographies again, as the Alexandrians did, to describe in detail the human face and form, to collect strange animals and even strange people. It is in keeping with this taste that the sketch-books of Jacopo Bellini, of Leonardo, of Pisanello, and of their contemporaries are filled with drawings of animals, flowers, clouds, mountains, and other natural things.

But "fidelity to nature" is a notoriously equivocal formula. The multiple meanings of "nature" and its derivatives have been discriminated by A. O. Lovejoy and we shall not attempt to expand upon his treatment of the

[8] As early as 1493 Bellincioni had written a sonnet on another portrait by Leonardo, that of Cecilia Gallerani, the mistress of Ludovico Sforza. The sonnet plays upon the rivalry between art and nature and begins,

> Di chi ti adiri? A chi invidia Natura?
> Al vince che ha ritratto una tua stella . . .

(For the whole sonnet, see *Le Rime di Bernardo Bellincioni*, ed. by Pietro Fanfani, Bologna, 1878.) The idea is, of course, a literary commonplace and for that very reason of peculiar interest. The portrait, it may be added, seems to have disappeared. A similar idea is found in the Latin verses on a portrait of Lucrezia Crivelli in *The Notebooks of Leonardo da Vinci*, 1938, II, 394.

subject.[9] But we must notice what the phrase meant to
Vasari and earlier to Leonardo. In the passage quoted
from the biographer and critic, one observes that the
artist is praised for reproducing the likeness of his sitter as
Apelles is said to have reproduced the likeness of his
grapes. Just as the birds in the classical instance pecked at
the painted grapes, so the observer of the *Mona Lisa* believes the original to be before him, with beating pulses and
living eyes. But before the passage is over one finds that
Leonardo is praised also for painting the woman with a
pleasant and smiling expression, as she appeared when
listening to cheerful music or jesting talk; so that " while
looking at it one thinks it rather divine than human."

How much literary exaggeration is expressed in these
last words and how much they echo a Neoplatonic strain
is hard to tell. Even in Leonardo, whose interest in reproducing natural objects led to those amazing anatomical
and botanical and geological drawings, there are Neoplatonic elements. If he says, on the one hand, " Wisdom
is the daughter of experience," and backs it up with
minutely detailed studies of what he observes, he says on
the other, " Nature is full of infinite causes which were
never set forth in experience." [10] If he says, " O marvellous
Necessity, thou with supreme reason constrainest all effects to be the direct result of their causes, and by a supreme and irrevocable law every natural action obeys thee
by the shortest possible process," he also says, " Nature
being capricious and taking pleasure in creating and producing a continuous succession of lives and forms. . . ." [11]

[9] See *Primitivism in Antiquity*, pp. 447 ff., and " Nature as Aesthetic Norm," *Mod. Lang. Notes*, XLII (1927), pp. 444 ff.

[10] *Notebooks*, I, 85 and 77, respectively.

[11] *Ibid.*, I, 253 and 80 respectively. For a denial of the presence of

Which of these Natures he saw as he drew his sketches, there is now no saying. But the probability is that most of his contemporaries saw in the sketches after they were drawn the capriciously creative and fertile Nature rather than the mechanistic and purely geometrical. For a hundred or more years after Vasari there is little or no mention of the *Mona Lisa*. According to the French historian, Lemonnier,[12] Leonardo and his Italian *confrères* who were called to France by Francis I " furent traités avec toutes sortes d'égards et reçurent des appointements en rapport avec leur réputation." There was even circulated the old story that Leonardo died in the King's arms, a story now discredited.[13] But although more of his authentic pictures belonged to the crown—and now to the French Republic—than to any other single collector, most French writings of the sixteenth, seventeenth, and even eighteenth centuries are silent about him.[14] He is not mentioned in the letters of Marguerite d'Angoulême,[15] in the works of Rabelais, Montaigne—not even in his *Journal de Voyage*—nor the Pleiade; the courtiers, who might have seen at least the *Mona Lisa*, say nothing that we have been able to discover of either the picture or its author;

Neoplatonism in Leonardo, see E. Panofsky, *Studies in Iconology*, 1939, p. 182.

[12] In Lavisse's *Histoire de France*, V, i, 316.

[13] See L. Roger-Milès, *op. cit.*, pp. 15 f. The story, as is well known, dates from the time of Vasari.

[14] Though Poussin drew the illustrations for the edition of the *Trattato* which appeared in the middle of the seventeenth century, Leonardo was not so highly esteemed as Raphael, for instance, or even some of the lesser painters. *Cf.* A. Fontaine, *Les doctrines d'art en France*, 1909, p. 3.

[15] The sister of his great French patron, who, according to Roger-Milès, *op. cit.*, p. 65, is portrayed in Leonardo's (?) *Marriage of Saint Catherine*.

even Louis Leroy, whose *De la Vicissitude ou variété des choses de l'univers* (1579) lists the painters whose works have raised his times to eminence, omits Leonardo's name. One possible reason for this is that the *Mona Lisa* belonged to the King and therefore not many people had the chance to see it. But the most famous pictures and sculptures of the time were made familiar to the interested public by engravings, and if Leonardo had captured the imagination of Frenchmen, his works would doubtless have been both known and spoken of, as those of Raphael were.[16]

In the middle of the seventeenth century, Leonardo's name and the *Mona Lisa* emerge once more. Père Dan, who made a catalogue of the works of art at Fontainebleau, calls it the *premier en estime, comme une merveille de la peinture.*[17] In whose estimation it ranked first and why it was considered a marvel are not recealed. Félibien, somewhat later, continues the Vasari tradition.

This is one of the most finished of his works. It is said that he took so much pleasure in working on it that he spent four months on it, and that while he was painting this lady there was always someone near her who sang or played some musical instrument, so as to keep

---

[16] The portrait could only have been seen by persons admitted to the " gilt cabinet " at Fontainebleau, which would have required special permission. It was removed to Versailles by Louis XIV, probably after 1694, the last date on which it appears in the inventories of Fontainebleau (See *La Grande Encyclopédie*, XVIII, p. 950). It was not exhibited in the Louvre until after the Revolution. It does not appear to have been engraved until the nineteenth century. For its history in France, see the catalogue of the Louvre by Georges Lafenestre and Eugène Richtenberger, tr. by B. H. Dausseron, p. 56.

[17] *Trésor des Merveilles de Fontainbleau* (1642), quoted by Rigollet, *Cat. de l'oeuvre de Léonard de Vinci*, 1849, pp. 652 ff. Cassiano del Pozzo in 1625 saw the painting and commented on its bad condition. See Müntz, *Léonard de Vinci*, 1899, p. 421.

her joyful and prevent her from assuming that melancholy air which comes over one easily when one is inactive and motionless.

Truly, said Pymandre, if I may give my opinion, the time which he put into it was well spent, for I have never seen anything more finished or more expressive. There is so much grace and so much sweetness in the eyes and features of this face, that it appears to be alive. When one looks at this portrait, one would say it was a real woman who takes pleasure in being seen.

It is true, I replied, that Leonardo appears to have taken particular care to finish it well. And Francis I considered this picture to be one of the most finished products of this painter, wished to own it, and paid four thousand *écus* for it.[18]

The excellence of Leonardo's artistry is judged in this passage by its " finish " in the representation of a gentle and sweet woman's face. The time given to the work, four months, becomes a matter of the greatest interest to subsequent critics, who vary it as they will. Vasari had said that Leonardo " loitered " over it for four years—not months—and then had left it unfinished. Lanzi, pointing out the unfinished state of most of Leonardo's pictures, continues by saying that the impression of lack of finish is attributable to the artist's having left certain portions of his pictures less perfectly finished than others. This deficiency, he says, cannot be detected always by the best judges. "The portrait, for instance, of Mona Lisa Gioconda, . . . was minutely examined by Mariette in the collection of the king of France, and was declared to be carried to so high a degree of finish that it was impossible surpass it." [19] Stendhal passes on the story, saying that

[18] André Félibien, *Entretiens sur les vies et sur les ouvrages des plus excellens Peintres anciens et modernes*, 2d ed., 1685-1688, I, 193 f.

[19] Luigi Lanzi, *The History of Painting in Italy*, tr. by Thomas Roscoe, new ed. rev., 1853. The history was first published in 1789 and was considered for many years authoritative. It was translated and revised by the Reverend G. W. D. Evans in 1848. In translation

the artist "never considered it finished." [20] Delecluze reduces the time to three years.[21] The story continues to our own day through Houssaye, the American Moses F. Sweetser, his contemporary, Mrs. Charles W. Heaton, Gabriel Séailles, Mantz, Edward McCurdy, E. V. Lucas, and even Elbert Hubbard.[22]

II

For some three hundred years no one appears to have seen anything mysterious about this painting. It was the portrait of a certain merchant's wife in a cheerful mood, and what was found extraordinary in it was its fidelity to nature. But a merchant's wife is still a woman, and women began to occupy a curious position in many early nineteenth-century minds. They had previously been cruel, coquettish, vain, deceitful, gentle, fickle, tender, weak, but they had rarely been enigmatic. On the contrary, men knew them only too well. But the early nineteenth century introduced a new woman into the history of ideas— *la femme fatale.*[23]

the passage appears, "the labor of four years, and, after all, left unfinished." Mariette was the author of the *Abecedario de Pierre Jean Mariette*, which I have not seen.

[20] *Hist. de la Peinture en Italie*, 1817, I, 223 f.

[21] *Léonard de Vinci*, 1841, p. 29.

[22] See respectively, *Hist. de Léonard de Vinci*, pp. 439 ff.; *Leonardo da Vinci*, Boston, 1879, p. 59; *Leonardo da Vinci and his Works*, 1874, p. 51 f.; *Léonard de Vinci*, 1892, p. 140; *Leonardo da Vinci*, 1898, II, 158; *Leonardo da Vinci*, 1904, p. 113; *Leonardo da Vinci*, 1926, p. 9; *Little Journeys to the Homes of Eminent Artists*, 1902, X, ii, p. 46. Elbert Hubbard translated the sum of 4000 *scudi* into eighty thousand dollars. Stendhal had been content with forty five thousand francs.

[23] This is, of course, a commonplace, but see Mario Praz, *The Romantic Agony*, 1933, ch. IV, esp. pp. 243 ff. The reader also would do well to complete what follows in our text by pursuing Mr. Beren-

The *femme fatale* emerged with Romanticism. She was all sensation and feeling, as against masculine rationality. She captured men by her apparent passivity, lying in wait like a fascinating serpent for the flitting bird who was the male. Whether the Romanticists knew it or not, she could trace her ancestry back to the Eve of Philo Judaeus. The Romantic critics, whether they were engaged in interpreting paintings or poetry, treated their works of art as if they were hieroglyphs. Each had a hidden " meaning " which only the initiated could uncover. To be one of the initiated, one must have a peculiar kind of sensitivity, an eye that not merely saw the perceptual screen of things but penetrated to something called the reality behind it. Such metaphors in practice meant that the critic was not to record what he saw, but to let his imagination freely play about the work of art and to report what it constructed.

What Vasari was for the pre-nineteenth century critic, Théophile Gautier and Walter Pater became for their contemporaries and successors. Both started a tradition—in apparent independence of each other—which has not died even to-day. Gautier's paragraph was the earlier published.

Leonardo da Vinci retained the finesse of the Gothic period while animating it with a spirit entirely modern. . . . The faces of Vinci seem to come from the upper spheres to be reflected in a glass or rather in a mirror of tarnished steel, where their image remains eternally fixed by a secret similar to that of the daguerreotype. We have seen these faces before, but not upon this earth: in some previous existence perhaps, which they recall to us vaguely. How explain otherwise the strange, almost magic charm which the portrait of Mona Lisa has for even the least enthusiastic natures? Is it her

son's suggestion of the influence of Lavater and the other physiognomists. See his *The Study and Criticism of Italian Art*, 1916, p. 24.

beauty? Many faces by Raphael and other painters are more correct. She is no longer even young; her age must be that loved by Balzac, thirty years; through the subtle modelling we divine the beginnings of fatigue, and life's finger has left its imprint on this peachlike cheek. Her costume, because of the darkening of the pigments, has become almost that of a widow; a crêpe veil falls with the hair along her face; but the expression, wise, deep, velvety, full of promise, attracts you irresistibly and intoxicates you, while the sinuous, serpentine mouth, turned up at the corners, in the violet shadows, mocks you with so much gentleness, grace, and superiority, that you feel suddenly intimidated, like a schoolboy before a duchess. The head with its violet shadows, seen as through black gauze, arrests one's dreams as one leans on the museum railing before her, haunts one's memory like a symphonic theme. Beneath the form *expressed*, one feels a thought which is vague, infinite, *inexpressible*, like a musical idea. One is moved, troubled, images *already seen* pass before one's eyes, voices whose note seems familiar whisper languorous secrets in one's ears; repressed desires, hopes which drive one to despair stir painfully in the shadow shot with sunbeams; and you discover that your melancholy arises from the fact that la Joconde three hundred years ago greeted your avowal of love with this same mocking smile which she retains even to-day on her lips.[24]

Here simple fidelity to nature has completely disappeared; the eternal feminine has taken its place. The *Mona Lisa* is not the portrait of a young woman; she has ripened through experience. She recalls past lives, stirs up repressed desires, mocks you with her smile. At once a new strain enters into French criticism. Whereas the earlier critics had seen sweetness and gentleness, the later began to see something more troubling. Even Taine, who was scarcely a victim of "the Romantic agony," found the famous smile "doubting, licentious, Epicurean, deliciously tender, ardent, sad," and united it to the smiles

[24] Théophile Gautier *et al.*, *Les Dieux et les demi-dieux de la peinture*, [1863], p. 24 f. The article on Leonardo first appeared in 1858. For further information about it, see Spoelberch de Lovenjoul, *Hist. des oeuvres de Théophile Gautier*, pp. 160, 262 ff.

of the Saint John, the Saint Anne, and other Vincian
smiles.[25] Houssaye, one of the co-authors of Gautier's
book, who was interested enough in facts to write a Life of
Leonardo, also is captivated by the new mystery. He feels
it his duty to bring in her " charm, provocative and ineffable, cruel and divine, sybilline and voluptuous." [26] This
diabolical charm appears also, somewhat intensified, in
Charles Blanc and Paul Mantz.

Before a painting so wonderful and so admired, the time which was
consumed in painting it is explained either by the fact that the artist
experienced the fascination which he has so well expressed, and
prolonged as far as possible the sweets of conversation with this
charming woman, or that he had difficulty in expressing the proud
serenity and restrained provocation of this face whose smile, at certain
moments, seems satanic and still magnetises us by its long and
voluptuous glances. It seems that after having carried the modelling
to the point of the most delicate shading, to imperceptible accents, and
thus brought it close to us by palpitating truth, the artist may have
desired then to withdraw it into the mystery of half-light, to hold it
remote from our gaze by shrouding it in a gauze and to make it appear as a dream amid a wild landscape, against an unbelievable background of little mountains, blue, rocky, pointed, cut from crystal,
and like stalactites turned upwards towards the skies.[27]

All that was lacking now was an explanation of the
mysterious charm of this face. The explanation must lie,
according to romantic procedure, in the life of the painter,
and it was not hard to find reasons for believing that the
original Lisa was the mistress of the painter.[28] Charles

[25] H. Taine, *Voyage en Italie*, 1902 (1st ed. 1865), II, 409.

[26] Arsène Houssaye, *op. cit.*, p. 125.

[27] *Hist. des peintres de toutes les écoles. Ecole Florentine*, 1879.
See p. 27 f. for the full account. It is typical of writers of this school
that they will say, " stalactites turned upwards towards the skies "
rather than " stalagmites."

[28] *Michelangelo, Leonardo da Vinci and Raphael*, tr. by Louisa
Corhan, (n. d.), pp. 201 ff.; French ed. 1861. A poem on the same

Clément told the extraordinary story in full. He noticed, he says, that whereas the men's heads by Leonardo were all individualized, those of the women were all identical. On a panel belonging to the Orleans family was discovered a reclining female whose features were those of *La Gioconda*. In the Fesch Collection and in the Hermitage are two half-length nudes with the same face. The original Lisa was the third wife of Giocondo—so that her husband must have been much older than she. Leonardo was young, witty and handsome when he painted her. The portrait at which " he worked or pretended to work " for four years never became the property of her husband. Finally, it is from the time when he painted the *Mona Lisa* that the other female heads begin to resemble hers.

As a matter of cold fact it requires no deep observation of Leonardo's portrait to see how little it resembles the Saint Anne and the Saint John and the various Madonnas. The one common character is the smile, but the series of thirty or more archaic maidens in the Acropolis museum in Athens have an identical smile, which they share with many other archaic statues of both men and women. Are we to conclude from this anything except that such smiles were the fashion of the times? Leonardo's saints and other supernatural beings do resemble one another; he gave them a certain " ideal " head. But the portraits attributed to him are individualized. The face of the *Mona Lisa* cannot be said to resemble the face of *La Belle Ferronière*, if that portrait be indeed by him. And neither of them closely resembles his saints.

Pater's famous passage on our painting is of course better known to English readers than Gautier's, and was

theme was produced by M. A. Dollfus and may be found in Houssaye, *op. cit.*, pp. 335 f.

perhaps the source of most later American and English interpretations of it. Pater suggests more than he states, whether from timidity, ignorance, or critical principle, but one may vaguely discern through his poetic prose that, like Clément, he finds a disconcerting similarity running through all the female heads and, like Gautier, a symbol of metempsychosis. The symbolism, he maintains, is not " crude," but the picture has " a subdued and grace-ful mystery." He believes that the " unfathomable smile, always with a touch of something sinister in it," plays over all of Leonardo's work. " From childhood we see this image defining itself on the fabric of his dreams; and but for express historical testimony, we might fancy that this was but his ideal lady, embodied and beheld at last." He suggests a fusion of his dream and the real Mona Lisa. And then follows the purple passage which has been re-printed even in anthologies of poetry. In that face " strange thoughts and fantastic reveries and exquisite passions " are " deposited cell by cell " upon the flesh. " All the thoughts and experiences of the world have been etched and moulded there, in that they have of power to refine and make expressive the outward form, the animal-ism of Greece, the lust of Rome, the reverie of the middle age with its spiritual ambition and imaginative loves, the return of the Pagan world, the sins of the Borgias." Mona Lisa becomes the " fancy of perpetual life," a rein-carnation of Leda, Helen, Saint Anne.[29]

[29] Walter Pater, *The Renaissance*, 1st ed., 1873. The essay itself was first published in the *Fortnightly Review*, Nov. 1869, pp. 494 ff. Donald A. Stauffer, in an interesting article, *Monna Melancholia* (*Sewanee Review*, XL, 89 ff.) gives reasons for believing that Pater had never seen the original of the *Mona Lisa* and had superimposed Dürer's *Melancholy I* upon it in his memory. For intimations of an influence of Gautier on Pater through Swinburne, called to my at-

Few art critics of the nineteenth century, capable of reading Pater, resisted his musical style, and we find dozens of imitators of him in the years that followed the publication of *The Renaissance.* Mrs. Charles W. Heaton, for instance, saw in the portrait, " a sweet but perplexing poem," and a visible embodiment of " the words of the preacher, ' vanitas vanitatum.' " [30] Mr. Frank Preston Stearns, after a passage on the " meaning " of the smile, dwélls upon the sense of mystery in Leonardo's character, which is " expressed without reservation " in this picture.[31] Elbert Hubbard, in one of his *Little Journeys*, brought in the words of the Preacher, as well as those of Walter Pater, added Cleopatra to Leda, Helen, and Saint Anne, and filled three pages with an eloquent description of a smile which he called " ineffable." [32] Mr. George B. Rose expressed the usual thoughts about the " inscrutability " of the smile, " a smile that is only on the lips, while in the eyes there are unsounded depths. Vainly we question her; like the Sphinx her riddle eludes us still." [33] Mr. Edward

tention by Professor Meyer Schapiro, see Louise Rosenblatt, *L'Idée de l'art pour l'art etc.*, 1931, p. 105.

[30] *Leonardo da Vinci and his Works*, 1874, p. 52.

[31] *The Midsummer of Italian Art*, 1895, p. 60. Though the Notebooks had not as yet been published when Mr. Stearns's book appeared, the *Treatise on Painting* alone might have shown him that Leonardo was enamored more of precision and clarity than of mystery.

[32] *Little Journeys to the Homes of Eminent Artists*, X, no. 2, pp. 46-50, (Feb. 1902). Hubbard's opinion of the picture may not seem important; but he was considered a great authority on " culture " by the general public of his day. The circulation of his *Little Journeys* was always large and his writings must have been the source of the aesthetic of many unschooled Americans.

[33] *The World's Leading Painters*, 1912, p. 50. In a similar vein Laura Spencer Porter conveyed to the ladies of America the " meaning " of the *Mona Lisa* in the *Woman's Home Companion*, April, 1914, (XLI, p. 54.)

McCurdy, after an analysis of the details of the portrait, concludes, " Thus, on the very confines of fantasy, and girt about with suggestions of strange lights and furtive shadows, he has created in this portrait of Madonna Lisa, third wife of a Florentine official, a myth of the embodiment of which men dream as of the eternal enigma of womanhood." [34]

III

From Gautier and Pater, as is clear, runs a tradition which is the very opposite of that started by Vasari. Whereas the Italian biographer and critic chiefly saw in the *Mona Lisa* a wonderful technical feat, the reproduction of a natural object, the French and English " aesthetes " saw it as a hieroglyph which required not simply contemplation but deciphering. It would appear to have become second nature to think of a picture—at least of this picture—as something of a rebus, a symbol whose meaning could be discovered only by a critic's intuition. That this school of writers attributed their theory of artistry to the artists whose works interested them need surprise no one. Critics are in the habit of reading an artist's mind.

This habit became strengthened when the psychology of Sigmund Freud achieved popularity. The nineteenth and twentieth centuries have been noteworthy, among other things, for a peculiar paradox: a combination of great

[34] *Leonardo da Vinci*, 1904, pp. 115 f. It is interesting to observe that James Jackson Jarves, the American collector and critic, who alone of the writers cited—and many others not cited—knew the Italian painters of the Renaissance intimately, was almost unique in his time in continuing the Vasari tradition rather than what we have called the Romantic. See his *Art Studies of the Old Masters of Italy*, 1861, I, p. 400.

scientific accomplishment with anti-intellectualism. Early in the former century, Schopenhauer began to argue that the understanding was created by the will to serve its own ends, an argument which he sought to deduce from Kantian principles. These ends, however, were not those of Kant's Practical Reason; they were, on the contrary, purely biological; and it was easy for Schopenhauer's successors to identify them with sexual ends. An artist, according to Freud, is a man whose sexual frustrations are released symbolically in pictures or statues or other works of art. Appetites which would never pass the Censor if expressed in their true nature, are permitted to appear in disguise.

As is well known, according to this theory the fundamental appetite of the human male is his love for his mother, known as the Oedipus Complex. Since incest in most Occidental society is not encouraged, the Oedipus Complex can only be released through art, and hence a Freudian critic will be likely to see in a picture a symbol of the artist's passion for his mother. Here, it will be observed, the critic assumes that the artist is not communicating something to the observer—he is really concealing something from the observer—but unconsciously expressing something of himself. When this something is revealed, it does not mean that the picture will be liked any the more; no standard of aesthetic judgment is implied in the psychoanalysis of a work of art. But it is clear that what mainly interests a Freudian, in any such work, will be the discovery of the unconscious motive. Freud's interpretation follows.

It was quite possible that Leonardo was fascinated by the smile of Mona Lisa because it had awakened something in him which had slumbered in his soul for a long time, in all probability an old memory.[35] This memory was of sufficient importance to stick to him once it had been aroused; he was forced continually to provide it with new expression. The assurance of Pater that we can see an image like that of Mona Lisa defining itself from Leonardo's childhood on the fabric of his dreams, seems worthy of belief and deserves to be taken literally.

Vasari mentions as Leonardo's first artistic endeavors, " heads of women who laugh." The passage, which is beyond suspicion, as it not meant to prove anything, reads more precisely as follows: " He formed in his youth some laughing feminine heads out of lime, which have been reproduced in plaster, and some heads of children, which were as beautiful as if modeled by the hands of a master. . . . "

Thus we discover that his practice of art began with the representation of two kinds of objects, which would perforce remind us of the two kinds of sexual objects which we have inferred from the analysis of his vulture phantasy. If the beautiful children's heads were reproductions of his own childish person, then the laughing women were nothing else but reproductions of Caterina, his mother, and we are beginning to have an inkling of the possibility that his mother possessed that mysterious smile which he lost, and which fascinated him so much when he found it again in the Florentine lady. . . . [36]

Not only is Freud able to construct a part of the hidden life of Leonardo from the *Mona Lisa*, he is also able to build up the life of the artist's mother. Since she was not married to Piero da Vinci, she was forced to " compensate herself for not having a husband."

In the manner of all ungratified mothers she thus took her little son in place of her husband, and robbed him of a part of his virility by the too early maturing of his eroticism. . . . When in the prime of his life Leonardo re-encountered that blissful and ecstatic smile as it had once encircled his mother's mouth in caressing, he had long been under the ban of an inhibition forbidding him ever again to

---

[35] According to Vasari, the smile had to be artificially produced and preserved.

[36] Sigmund Freud, *Leonardo da Vinci*, 1916, pp. 85 ff. There is no objective evidence that Caterina resembled Lisa, in smile or otherwise.

desire such tenderness from women's lips. But as he had become a painter he endeavored to reproduce this smile with his brush and burnish all his pictures with it, whether he executed them himself or whether they were done by his pupils under his directions, as in Leda, John, and Bacchus.[37]

The way was now open for further embroidering on this psychological background, and critics were not slow to follow it. Pictures became clues to the subconscious labyrinths of an artist's mind. Regardless of the fact that this particular picture seemed to have been painted as a portrait, which might lead one to suppose that its appearance was to a large extent determined by the attributes of the woman who sat for it, its main interest was now held to lie in what it could tell us about the man who made it. This shift in critical attention was the kind of reversal of opinion best illustrated in the Hegelian dialectic. Whereas in Vasari the picture was considered with reference to its closeness to the objective world of nature, in Freud it is considered as a disclosure of the most intimately subjective world, the so-called Unconscious. But since the world which it reveals can be known only by means of a theory which is applied to the particular object, rather than one which has been deduced from it, the critic has only to make up his mind what was in the artist's Unconscious and then discover it spread out before him in the picture.

One finds a still more remarkable example of this in the volume written on our artist by Rachel Annand Taylor, *Leonardo the Florentine.* For her the *Mona Lisa* is a phase in Leonardo's transition from concealment to avowal of his homosexuality. It is, she says,[38] " as if he

[37] *Ibid.*, p. 91 ff.

[38] Rachel Annand Taylor, *Leonardo the Florentine*, 1927, esp. pp. 350-354. Only one who has gone through the whole of this book can get its full flavor.

were afraid to see his Narcissus except in a disguise." Presumably when he painted his Saint John, he was no longer ashamed to see his Narcissus. But even if he were not, it is hardly likely that he painted the picture in order to inform the world that he had conquered his shame. This becomes doubly true if one accepts the Freudian theory that art is always a symbolical rather than a literal satisfaction of repressions.

Happily, we are not engaged in an examination of Freudianism. Our purpose is simply to indicate how it reoriented aesthetic comment on this picture in the twentieth century. A writer now feels it possible to assume that a painter is painting for himself rather than for an observer, and that, if an observer should present himself before a picture, he should find in it what the artist himself concealed in it. But since only initiated Freudians know what is concealed in pictures, the uninitiated observer fails to see what the picture really is, or " means." He is in the position of a European ignorant of Chinese looking at Chinese characters and thinking they are merely patterns.

If the *Mona Lisa* at the present time is considered old-fashioned, that is probably to be attributed more to the writings of the Gautier-Pater school than to those of the psycho-analysts. Leonardo himself is far from old-fashioned; but it is now the scientific and philosophical Leonardo rather than the artistic. This paper is not concerned with the decline of interest in the painting, but we may be permitted to suggest that M. Paul Valéry is probably right in saying that the association of " mystery " with the picture has had more influence than any other one thing in disgusting people with it.[39]

[39] See his *Leonardo da Vinci*, 1929, p. 58. For other hostile criticisms of this celebrated picture, see Berenson's *The Study and Criticism of*

The tendency in the criticism of painting from about 1910 to the beginning of sur-realism has been technical. It has consisted largely in studies of form, color, drawing. Only since Marxian criticism became fashionable has there been much attention paid to subject-matter. But in such criticism little is said of adequacy of representation—fidelity to " nature "; the critic is concerned only with the " social significance " of the work of art. Hence to such critics, the *Mona Lisa* would have no great interest, unless, perhaps, as an illustration of the rise of the middle class, for the lady so carefully portrayed was probably a *bourgeoise*.

It may not be inappropriate to terminate with a celebrated passage from the artist's note-books about the portraiture of women. " Women," Leonardo says, " should be represented in modest attitudes with legs close together, arms folded, and their heads low and bending sideways." [40] The head of La Gioconda is not bending sideways, but otherwise the precept appears to be carried out in the painting. Add to it the memorandum on the importance of painting faces in a nebulous light, and you begin to have a clue to his method of portraiture. This will throw no light on what is " expressed " by the picture, nor is that, fortunately, our affair. We know that Leonardo was attracted by chiaroscuro and busy with the

Italian Art, pp. 3 f.; A. C. Barnes, *The Art in Painting*, 1925, p. 368; P. Dearmer, " Leonardo da Vinci, a Criticism," *Contemporary Review*, Vol. 135 (1929), p. 217. The Italian Futurists, in their campaign to liberate Italian art from the museum-pieces, quite naturally attacked it. A good example may be found in Soffici's *Giornale di Bordo*, 1915, p. 147: " In tram.—Vedo scritto su un muro a grandi lettere bianche su fondo blu: GIOCONDA: ACQUA PURGATIVA ITALIANA. E piu giù la faccia melensa di Monna Lisa. Finalmente. Ecco che si comincia anche da noi a far della buona critica artistica."

[40] *The Notebooks of Leonardo da Vinci*, p. 240.

means of utilizing it. We may fittingly leave to phychia-
trists the problem why such things interested him.

Our purpose in this paper has been merely to show how
a given work of art may in different periods have essentially different content—and therefore be admired for different, if not for contradictory, reasons. If this instance is
typical, it would appear that works of art which " with-
stand the test of time " change their natures as the times
change. The work of art becomes thus the locus of a new
set of values determined by the preconceptions or the predominant interest of the new critic or observer.

INDEX

(The Index lists almost all the proper names and subjects which occur in the body of the book. Exceptions are references made in passing which, in the opinion of the author, would not be likely to be remembered. The names of all works of art are in italics, whether books or not. But the names of characters in books and plays are in Roman. Only the page on which a discussion begins is listed.)